WHY LEADERS ARE GIFTING 1
TO ALL THEIR PEOPLE!

"We support an industry that is under tremendous pressure from an increasing number of complex challenges. In an effort to support their communities, our customers are expected to operate with limited margin for error—which takes a huge toll on the mental health and well-being of the very people we rely upon to innovate and execute. Dr. G's strategies, sense of humor and down-to-earth relatability have profoundly and reliably helped our employees and customers continue to make positive change. This book provides a comprehensive user's manual that will help your team embrace change as an opportunity to excel by becoming more resilient, both personally and professionally."

-Peter Londa, President & CEO Tantalus Systems

"Dr. G never fails to astound and inspire audiences. She's been with us on *The Doctors* for four seasons now and her ability to explain complex topics in a clear and accessible way is only one of the reasons we keep bringing her back. I'm so glad her next book is here—it's going to help everyone who reads it to strengthen their own mental health, stop feeling overwhelmed, and be able to actually love their life."

-Patricia Ciano, Executive Producer, *The Doctors*

"Building a high-performing team requires a high-performing leader to 'think human.' As business leaders we are hearing and seeing all kinds of real human struggles from our people—both within their work and outside it. Dr. G has the science and the strategies to reframe experiences so that each person taps into their abilities to meet challenges while actually enjoying their life. The concepts in this book deliver a set of tools high-performing teams can and should consider using to optimize their performance inside and outside of the office."

-Doug Zarkin, Chief Marketing Officer, Pearle Vision

"*From Stressed to Resilient* is exactly the tool I want each of my clients to use and share with their team. Many people fear success because of the change it brings. Dr. Gilboa delivers the steps to strengthen individuals and teams so they can effectively navigate the stress that accompanies bigger goals and more achievement."

-Patty Block, Founder & President, The Block Group Inc.

"The pressures of the last few years have been unrelenting. Dr. G has the strategies to combat the burnout and stress faced by so many talented professionals—that's why I recommend her wisdom to my smartest, most forward-thinking client companies. Her approach, data, and humor make individuals and teams more effective in the midst of stress and change. Get one of these books for every member of your team!"

-Michael Law, Founder & CEO, Summit Strategy Group;
Founding Partner IBEX Partners

"When I need to 'wow' a big client, I often find myself tapping Dr. G for her strategic insights, her down-to-earth approach, and her powerful content. Her expertise is the wisdom that they didn't know they needed—until they meet her and discover that it's actually quite impactful to uncover the utility of stress while abandoning the havoc stress all too often wreaks. She helps brands navigate the ever-changing consumer landscape impacted by shrinking budgets, limited staff, and increasing burnout. What she offers goes far beyond just solutions, and instead gives us the tools and the strategies to build successful, resilient teams."

-Kevin Tressler-Gelok, Senior Vice President, MSL

"As a leading youth development authority in North America, we see clearly the stress and pain *adults* are facing as they work to support, protect, and raise the next generations. There is no expert better than Dr. G to help us all in that important work. Her new book, *From Stressed to Resilient*, is filled with practical strategies to build our own strength and give us the tools we need to grow resilience in ourselves and every life we touch."

-Tom Rosenberg, President and CEO, American Camp Association

FROM STRESSED TO RESILIENT

THE GUIDE TO HANDLE *MORE*
AND FEEL IT *LESS*

DEBORAH GILBOA, MD

TO THOSE WHO'VE TAUGHT ME BEST
HOW TO BE RESILIENT IN MY OWN LIFE.

Building Connections—Jonathan Weinkle, the man who knows everyone because he cares about everyone

Setting Boundaries—Sharon Weil, who is the most expansively loving and carefully tending of humans

Opening to Change—Oren, my son, who meets the world with compassion, curiosity, and courage

Managing Discomfort—Rachele Harmuth, who knows a million ways to navigate what's hard while pushing through to the good

Setting Goals—Nadav, my son, who sets the highest expectations for himself and encourages us all to aim for our best selves

Finding Options—Jesse Rosen, who has never met a problem he couldn't solve, especially when it means helping others

Taking Action—Ari, my son, who moves forward towards his purpose despite naysayers, obstacles, and the unknown

Persevering—Gavri, my son, who transforms the challenges he faces into strength and persistence to pursue his goals

…and my parents, for everything they didn't do for me because they believed in my ability to do it myself.

CONTENTS

CHAPTER 1

WE BELIEVE A LIE

WHAT'S THE LIE?

That stress is poison.

Does this sound familiar to you? "Stress is bad and bad for us!" We've been taught to fear stress—to avoid it, to minimize it, to eliminate it, to get away from it before it kills us. If you're causing stress in someone's life, you're the villain. If someone is causing stress in your life, that relationship is toxic—get out! If you're stressed, you'll never be happy.

In my twenty years as a physician, I have absolutely seen the toll that stress takes on the human body and mind. The damage can be fatal. So how can it possibly be a lie?

Because that idea—that stress is a poison and should be avoided at all costs—ignores reality and sets people up to fail.

In reality, all change brings stress. *All* change. Big change, like a new boss. Small change, like a cellphone upgrade. The change you hate, like a cancer diagnosis. The change you love, like a promotion. The change you predicted, like a child growing up and moving out. The change you could never have predicted, like a worldwide pandemic.

All change brings stress, and every day brings change.

If the only "cure" to the damage stress does to us is to avoid it, we're all going to fail!

About eleven years ago, I saw a patient I'd known for years: a middle-aged, college-educated, middle-class white woman with progressive multiple sclerosis. Her disease had worsened to the point that she used a motorized wheelchair with a toggle control at her chin to move the chair. She couldn't rely on her arms or legs for much of anything at all.

"How are you today?" I asked as I came into the exam room.

"Oh, just wonderful," she replied. "My grandbaby turned one this weekend—he's getting to be such a big boy. The flowers by my front door are blooming, and I'm going to that Friday night concert in the park this week!" We went on and had our visit, checking in about her multiple medications and serious health risks.

I don't think I would've thought much more about her attitude and well-being, except it was only a little bit later the same morning that I saw another middle-aged, college-educated, middle-class white woman in the room next door.

This woman was well. No mental health issues, no physical issues except for some mild, occasional low back pain.

"How are you today?"

"I'm terrible!" she answered. "It's . . . everything! My back! My work doesn't make *any* accommodations. My family just plans things, never thinking how it will be for me or if I'll feel well enough to join them . . ."

"Have you been having pain?" I asked.

"No! But I *could* be!" she replied.

And I went on to help her as best I might, but I also kept thinking, how do folks turn out more like the woman behind Door #1? How can I?

That woman certainly hadn't been able to avoid stress, and more was coming at her every day as her body failed her. If avoiding stress wasn't her answer, what was?

I'd been a doctor for more than a decade at this point, and I was trying to reconcile several observations:

1. People are afraid of anything "stressful" because they're afraid of the harm it will cause.
2. Individual resilience—the ability to navigate change and come through it with integrity and purpose—is a much better predictor of people's happiness than health or wealth or anything else I can find.
3. The people who are resilient have faced a *great* deal of stress in their lives.

It took the stark contrast between those two women to get the lesson from these observations through my thick skull, but once I started seeing this truth, I saw it *everywhere*. People I'd long admired had stories filled with professional and personal difficulty. Individuals who smiled often weren't without suffering. That person at work who seemed to have it easy and all together? They didn't.

And it wasn't just individuals.

Groups that worked together with respect and precision in the office or the hospital? They'd gone through the ringer together more than a few times to learn those skills.

Organizations serving people in the community, financially stable and flexible enough to meet ever-growing needs? They had faltered and struggled along the way.

Companies with incredible culture and products that stand the test of time? They'd been through so much stress and change that they were usually almost unrecognizable when compared to their original circumstances.

I finally realized that well-being and success aren't achieved through avoiding stress and running away from change.

Well-being and success are achieved through using stress and navigating change.

So I set out to learn what makes stress survivable and how to put it to work for people and teams.

CHAPTER 2

SO WHAT'S THE TRUTH?

STRESS IS LIKE EXERCISE.

For most of us, stress—and exercise—is no fun at all. We do our best to avoid it because it leaves us tired, hurting, and feeling out of shape. But it's the only way to get stronger.

What if I told you that I get out of breath walking up one flight of stairs? The first question is, am I well? If I'm not, I need help to manage my lung or heart or muscle issue. If I am healthy, though, and I want to be able to walk up ten steps without getting winded, then you know what I need to do.

Walk up more stairs.

The only way to build my strength is to do the exercise frequently enough to teach my body how to manage it. The truly amazing thing is that, within a week of walking stairs, I will adapt. I will not only be able to walk up that flight of stairs without losing my breath, I won't feel tired or sore the next day. On the contrary, I will have increased energy!

The exact same is true of stress and mental health.

Do you feel fatigued by the stresses you're managing? Exhausted even? That's totally understandable. You're dealing with so much. You want to be able to handle this level of stress without feeling winded, tired, sore.

My first question is:
ARE YOU WELL?

That was not a rhetorical question. Are you mentally well?

Do you have anxiety that interferes with your ability to take care of your normal daily activities? Or sadness or anger or guilt that get in the way of your usual interactions? Do you have trouble getting out of bed in the morning or go to bed half hoping you won't wake up tomorrow? Do you ever think the world would be better off without you in it? Do you use alcohol or drugs to help you get through the day or sleep at night? Do you suspect that you have a mental health issue that hasn't been addressed or that you don't have enough help managing?

If the answer to any of those questions is yes, I need you to grab your phone and do two things.

The first is to decide who to call. Not *if* you should call someone, but who. You're reading this book, which means that you really want—or someone you love has convinced you—to feel better. Do you need to call for emergency help? Or do you feel comfortable reaching out to your doctor? Is it a friend or loved one that you should tell about how you're doing? Call, right now. If they don't pick up, leave a clear message stating what's happening with you. Please.

The second is to set an alarm in your phone for two business days from now. Call it "Do I still need help?" It's too easy to let these hard conversations go. You're stronger than that, and you deserve more than that.

If you are mentally well, and you want to be able to handle the stress in your life without feeling hurt by it, then—believe it or not—stress is actually the best way to get there. However, you may need to pace yourself at first.

Listen, if I got up tomorrow and tried to run a marathon, I could absolutely die. That has happened to people, and I could definitely be one of those people! Too much exercise is dangerous, especially at first.

If you are experiencing too many stressors or too big a stress, you can certainly be damaged by that. You need support and a plan to slowly build your strength.

You can absolutely build your mental endurance so that you can handle more surprises, more change, even more difficulty. The amazing thing about mental fitness is that, just like physical fitness, you can not only learn to handle all those challenges, you can handle them without the fatigue and without the pain that you're currently experiencing.

Stress is like exercise—and this book is your strengthening plan.

CHAPTER 3

ALL CHANGE IS STRESSFUL

CHANGE IS HARD.

Change that shocks you, hurts you, or scares you is all around you, and everyone knows how awful it can be. But to understand the true struggle of change and conquer it, you have to understand that all change is hard. Even change you really want, even change you work for, even change you dream about!

About five a.m. on a Thursday morning at the end of May 2015, I woke up—if I slept at all—in an unfamiliar hotel room in New York City for what would definitely be the biggest change of my professional life.

I showered, got dressed, packed up my belongings, and went downstairs to catch my ride. A ride, mind you, that I had tried to refuse. My destination was five blocks away, and my overnight bag was on wheels. But my manager had said no—apparently you did not arrive to this opportunity on foot. So, when the 2015 Lincoln Town Car arrived, I was waiting. My driver looked like he'd come straight out of central casting. Five foot nine inches, stocky, black pants, white shirt, a big shock of silver hair, and—and I say this as somebody who was born in the Bronx—a Brooklyn accent that almost knocked me over. "You Doctah G? I thought you'd be oldah. Do dey know you look about twelve? Anyway, I'm Tommy. OK. In ya go!"

In the car, Tommy started to prep me for my interview. "Do ya know dese guys? Lemme tell you about 'em!" For the next fifteen minutes—because New York rush hour—he kept up a steady stream of information, suggestions, and advice. Just as I caught a glimpse of our destination, he said, "You ready?"

Um, no.

I was definitely not ready for this change. I'd spent four years reading, writing, researching, speaking, giving interviews, hustling, and dreaming about getting on national TV . . . and I was about to step out the door without any clue how I was supposed to survive two and a half minutes on TV, let alone use it to make a difference in the lives of the Five. Million. Viewers!

"See ya afterwards, Doc!"

I got ushered straight into hair and makeup.

I smiled, cooperated, went over my set notes, all the while, with a constant rush of fear in my head.

As soon as I opened my mouth, I was going to lose:

- everything I meant to say,
- my confidence,
- my family's admiration and love,
- all my credibility!

The segment producer came in and ran through the script with me, and I started to believe I might—possibly—remember what I planned to say.

They moved me from hair and makeup—calling out, "Whatever you do, don't touch ya face!"—to the control room.

My smile started to be tinged with a little panic.

It's OK, I reassured myself. This is not really happening.

- The segment before mine will run long and they'll cancel mine.
- They will have to bump my segment for breaking news (happens all the time).
- They'll realize I look twelve years old (thanks, Tommy!) and won't let me on the set.

I must have been mistaken about all this though, because they walked me back to the edge of the set.

And this was when I got really nervous. So obviously I focused on the really important things:

- These shoes are too tight. I'm going to trip.
- My nose itches—but don't touch your face!

- My heart is pounding louder than Michael Strayhan's voice. What if he asks me a question?

And I realized . . . I don't have to do this. I can just leave. I've never seen GMA put a gun to a guest's head, so there is nothing stopping me from running out the door as if none of this ever happened.

The intern motioned me onstage and I had to decide: Go or run?

I walked onto the set.

I smiled, I listened, I answered, and I had pretty much the most fun I've ever had in two and a half minutes in my entire professional life.

I got back into the Town Car, and as we drove through Central Park on our way to LaGuardia Airport, Tommy debriefed my appearance like the trained psychologist he obviously is. "You faced something hard. That's stressful."

I started to argue with him—how can it be "hard" to have your professional dream come true? Then I realized he was totally right. It was hard, and it was stressful, even while it was amazing.

CHAPTER 4

WHY OUR BRAINS HATE CHANGE

OUR BRAINS ARE WIRED TO DO ONE THING ABOVE ALL ELSE.

Keep us alive.

Since we are currently alive, our brains are really skeptical about change. All change. The good, the bad, the change we expect, and (especially) the change that surprises us.

A Tangent That Isn't Really a Tangent

Have you ever been in the front seat of a car when the driver hit the brakes? Your seat belt locked up, right?

Your seat belt locked up whether the driver was trying to avoid a big accident or just reaching into the back seat for a Coke. The seat belt locking mechanism is a safety measure connected to the brakes. It doesn't know (or care) if you were avoiding a pile-up or tapping the brakes in time to the music on the radio. Hit the brakes = lock the seat belt.

Back to the Brain

Just like your car's seat belt, your brain has a series of safety mechanisms. It's not that every change will kill you; it's that any change is a risk. So every change gets evaluated for loss, distrust, and discomfort.

Safety Mechanism #1: Loss

Every change that comes along is first evaluated for the damage it could do—even change we like!

Can you think of a change you really wanted in the past few years that actually happened? What was it?

_____

_____

_____

Imagine you've applied for a new job. It's better than your current job, pays more, and offers more of the support and opportunities you want. You apply, and wait. Interview, and wait. And then you get the call—you're hired!

Even while the relief or excitement or happiness is coursing through you, your brain stops and you think about what you'll lose.

"What if this hurts my family?" "My old co-workers might hate me!" "Will this new job take more time?" "What if no one at the new place likes me?" "I won't know how the new computer system works!" (Spoiler alert: That last one might be true.)

When you found out your good change was actually happening, how did you feel?

_____

What were you worried about losing?

_____

_____

_____

Safety Mechanism #2: Distrust

While the brain ticks through risks and losses, it also spreads distrust.

"Is this job offer for real?" and "What if I'm terrible at it and get fired?"

It's not bad that our brains do this. It usually feels awful, but it happens for a really good reason. Your brain is acting like your safety belt. It has one big job—to keep you from dying—and it doesn't really care how you feel.

When you found out your good change was actually happening, did you believe it?

_____

What didn't you trust about it?

_____

_____

_____

Safety Mechanism #3: Discomfort

Even once you believe a change is really happening, instead of thinking about what's great, your brain will try to focus on how uncomfortable this change will be. You'll notice first what's different, awkward, or hard for you about this new situation.

When that good change happened, what was uncomfortable for you about it?

_____

_____

_____

Don't let your brain fool you!!

According to a pre-pandemic Gallup poll,[1] a whopping 85 percent of employees are unhappy in their jobs. Why would so many people stay in jobs they don't like? Our brain's natural fear of change stems from a need to avoid all the potential loss and distrust and discomfort that can happen when we look for a new situation. That doesn't mean you should avoid all change!

When your brain notices a change, it focuses on possible losses and heightens the distrust and discomfort that you feel. These feelings can trick you into thinking the change must be bad for you. Your gut reaction seems to be telling you to stay away.

Nope.

Your brain is trying to hold you back from a move that could kill you, just like your seat belt is holding you in back from flying through the windshield . . . even though you were just trying to take off your jacket while sitting at a red light.

How Do You "Unlock the Seat Belt" in Your Brain?

Recognize that your brain is doing its job (don't be mad at yourself for your "negative" reaction to change). And then . . .

Breathe and think.

Brains hate change at first. But as soon as you slow down and think about the change, you'll be able to notice what's good about it, why you might want it, or how to live with it.

When that good change happened, how much time did you need to get past the worries about loss, the distrust, the discomfort?

_____

_____

_____

What helped you to focus on the good?

_____

_____

_____

CHAPTER 5

WHAT IS THE ANSWER TO ALL THIS STRUGGLE?

IT'S CLEAR THAT ALL CHANGE CAUSES STRESS. But I made the argument that stress can be useful, like exercise is (often awful, but also) useful. If stress is like exercise, and exercise builds body health, what does stress build?

Stress builds resilience!

Resilience is the ability to navigate change and come through it without being hurt by it. More than that, resilience is the ability to come through that change stronger and more whole and to navigate change with integrity and purpose.

Think about it. When we see someone who can handle difficulty, change, or surprises well, we say that person is resilient. So let me ask *you* (and brace yourself, because you're going to do a lot of the thinking in this book), what does resilience look like in people?

In your opinion (the only one that counts here) . . . What do resilient people *do*?
List some actions that you've seen people take when they were navigating change well: *Get more information* Talk to experts* Count to ten* Consider their options* Gather their team for discussion* What else??*

_____

_____

What do resilient people say? Name some things you've heard people say when they face difficulty:

"Can I have a little time to decide?"* "I need more information"* "What do you think?"* I'm considering our options"* "I've been through something like this before."* What else?

_____

_____

What do resilient people show? What attributes or behaviors or traits do you notice in people you see as resilient?

Adaptability* Strength* Calmness* Optimism* Caring* What else?

_____

_____

The *Oxford Advanced Learner's Dictionary*'s definition of resilience is "the ability of people or things to recover quickly after something unpleasant, such as shock, injury, etc."[1] Does that definition give a full picture of what you believe resilience to be? Can you expand or refine that definition to give yourself a more complete picture of what you want to do or be when you face a change? Write your own definition below.

Resilience (noun) ri-ZIL-y*uh*ns :

_____

_____

_____

Resilience is our goal because this means we are strong in the face of change and still true to our own personality, experience, and beliefs and that we can navigate whatever life throws at us or whatever we want to achieve without breaking. Not only without breaking—we can find happiness.

CHAPTER 6

LEARN RESILIENCE ON PURPOSE

FOR MANY YEARS, educators thought kids who struggled to read couldn't be helped. Therefore, students in the lowest reading group in kindergarten found themselves to always be in the lowest reading group.

In 2007, after decades of research, Carol Dweck called this way of looking at academic ability a "fixed mindset."[1] And then she showed how it's false.

It turns out that intelligence, creative ability, and even character can all grow in anyone at any time. For more than fifteen years, educators have been figuring out how to go beyond helping kids learn tasks and have discovered how to teach kids to learn more easily.

Just as they so often do with a person's ability to learn, people tend to have a fixed mindset about resilience. They believe that resilience is an attribute that you're born with, and that's it. If you're in the lowest group at age five, you'll always struggle. If you're lucky enough to be in the highest group, that's where you'll stay.

Also false.

Resilience is a growth commodity. This means you can grow it on purpose, and you can lose it by accident.

A couple of years ago, I was consulting for a corporation—building resilience skills in their leadership team and developing ways to grow resilience in the whole company.

A few months into our relationship, the CEO called me. "Hey, do you remember M?" He was referring to a woman on his exec team who was the go-to person if someone needed help. She'd demonstrated excellent resilience skills consistently in her time working there.

"Well, she's really struggling and I don't understand it. I'm hoping you can help," the CEO said.

One of the other executive team members had to take leave to care for his mom, who had been diagnosed with a serious cancer. They'd met as a group and redistributed his responsibilities among the rest of the team. Everyone was pretty successfully navigating the change, except M. "She keeps dropping the ball on his work and her own. She's aware of it, she feels terrible about it, but it's getting worse."

So the CEO, M, and I had a meeting. I encouraged him to be empathetic and curious, and here is what we learned. The cancer that this coworker's mother was facing was the exact same type of cancer that had killed M's mom a few years ago. Her colleague's struggle floored her, and she hadn't realized that her grief was preventing her from handling the change in responsibilities with anything close to her usual abilities.

Resilience can drop when we face too big a stressor or too many stressors at once. But, just like an injury from exercise, once you know what is happening you can address it, heal, and get back to training.

Much more often, resilience can grow!

It's time to dispel a myth: people mostly believe that resilience can grow—but only by surviving hardship. That's false, in two ways.

1. Not everyone gets more resilient when they face difficulties.
Think about it. You know someone who has faced lots of struggles but never seems to get any stronger or someone who seems constantly to be up against adversity, but it never gets any easier for them. Struggle is not enough—we need some context and some skills if we hope to learn from the useful lessons in the difficulties.

2. There are lots of ways to grow resilience without suffering.

This is where it gets really good. Keep reading!

CHAPTER 7

THE INGREDIENTS OF RESILIENCE

RESILIENCE CAN BE GROWN. FANTASTIC. BUT HOW?

After years of working with business leaders, entrepreneurs, and individuals, proving the case for intentionally building resilience, I came to this fundamental question.

Once we recognize—as you have—that resilience isn't just a character trait that you're either born with or not, that we can "train up" to handle more change and stress but feel it less, we need answers. What skills can we learn or improve on to become stronger?

There are several scientifically validated scales that researchers use to measure resilience. They ask for responses on a scale of disagree-to-agree for all types of statements, like:

- I tend to take a long time to get over setbacks in my life.
- I have good friends who support me (rate yes/sometimes/no).
- I seek out new knowledge.
- I set limits for myself.
- I can make unpopular or difficult decisions.

and many, many more.

These dozens and dozens of similarly themed questions investigate our ability to navigate change and come through it with integrity and purpose.

I examined these scientifically validated, evidence-based scales to find out what they were measuring. What do resilient people have that overwhelmed people don't?

The answer? Eight skills and eight attributes.

That's right—there are eight skills that people use to be resilient and eight attributes that help people face change without being damaged, running away, or freezing up.

Eight Resilience Skills:

1. Build connections
2. Set boundaries
3. Open to change
4. Manage discomfort
5. Set goals
6. Identify options
7. Take action
8. Persevere (keep trying)

Did you tick through that list and think, "I've done all those things!"? Excellent! Just about every adult has. That means you have a basis for all of those skills. Just like an athlete who wants to improve their performance, you already have the basics and probably excel in some of those areas.

This book is going to help you fill in the gaps. In the following sections, you're going to find activities you can do right now to develop and refine those skills. Even more importantly, you're going to connect what you already know to your own resilience—so that you can use the fundamentals you have to feel better right away.

Wait, what about the "attributes"?

I'm glad you (I) asked!

Resilience Attributes:

1. Adaptability
2. Sense of humor
3. Self-efficacy (the belief that one can successfully accomplish a task)
4. Empathy
5. Optimism
6. Confidence

7. Faith (in ideals)
8. Knowledge gained from past struggles and successes

Do you have a fixed mindset about any of those? Maybe you look at that list and think, for example, "Well, there's nothing I can do about my sense of humor. It is what it is." Or you assume you can't become more empathetic or more optimistic. Not so!

Certainly "past struggles and successes" are a fixed commodity in that they've already happened. However, a lot can change about how we see our past experiences, how we frame them for ourselves, speak about them, and learn from them.

While all of those attributes can be developed, if you choose, they develop more slowly than skills. Also, attributes shape our identity and sense of self in ways that skills most often do not. So in this book, we're going to build skills while we notice attributes.

Think about your attributes. Rate your comfort with each from "That doesn't seem like me at all" to "Definitely me!" Put your first initial on the line to indicate your comfort level with each trait at this point in your life.

Adaptability

(not like me at all)   (definitely me!)

Sense of Humor

(not like me at all)   (definitely me!)

Self-efficacy

(not like me at all)   (definitely me!)

Empathy

(not like me at all)   (definitely me!)

Optimism

(not like me at all)   (definitely me!)

Confidence

(not like me at all)   (definitely me!)

Faith (in ideals)

(not like me at all)   (definitely me!)

Knowledge Gained from Past Struggles and Successes

(not like me at all)   (definitely me!)

Traits change as we go through life, and we can strengthen the ones we want more of, but it's slow going. We're going to focus on the skills and see what happens to these traits at the same time.

What in the world does that mean? Read on. One more chapter in the introduction, and then we'll get into the action!

CHAPTER 8

HOW TO USE THIS BOOK

BUILD ANY OR ALL OF THE EIGHT RESILIENCE SKILLS. Grow the resilience attributes at the same time. That's the plan!

Reading Doesn't Actually Work

Reading about something can be enlightening. It can change the way you think or feel. To change your behavior, though, it turns out you have to actually do something.

That's Why . . .

In each section you'll read an explanation of the skill and how that "muscle" will strengthen your overall resilience. Then you'll find four activities, each one of which will grow that skill in you. Do one activity, a few, or all of them. That's up to you.

You can, of course, follow the sections in order, but you do not need to do that. Like any training plan, it works best when it fits your needs, so pick the skills you want or need most.

Consider the Eight Resilience Skills

Now put them in order for *you*, from hardest to easiest:
- Hardest, meaning the ones that you don't understand or that you struggle with the most. Move this to the number one spot.

- Easiest, meaning the ones that come naturally to you, that you already do, or that you feel most knowledgeable about and comfortable with. Move this to the number 8 spot.
- Move the rest to the #2–#7 spots according to your own competence at each from almost hardest to almost easiest.

1. Build connections	1.	
2. Set boundaries	2.	
3. Open to change	3.	
4. Manage discomfort	4.	
5. Set goals	5.	
6. Identify options	6.	
7. Take action	7.	
8. Persevere (keep trying)	8.	

Look at your "Hardest to Easiest" list. Why do you think the hardest ones are hardest for you? It might be because you don't see the value in those strengths, or you have a character trait that feels in conflict with that skill (for example, you love to help people and so setting boundaries seems in conflict with that), or you just haven't practiced those hardest skills much. It might be that you don't understand what the heck I mean by "open to change" or "identify options" or whatever.

Consider Your Own Stressors

Let me ask you a question on a (seemingly) different topic. Why did you open this book? What are the stresses you'd like to handle better but feel less? What big or recent changes are most stressful for you right now? What and who are you worried about in your life?

List the current struggles or changes you're dealing with right now:

_____

_____

_____

What Do You Need?

When you reflect on all the things that are causing you stress right now, what would help? Do you see how it might help to set better boundaries so that you don't feel like you are obligated to (and maybe resentful of) so many responsibilities? Do you wish you could feel less uncomfortable with a big change? Would you like support from others to help you take action with a difficult decision?

Put the resilience skills in order from "most useful" to "least necessary" for you today.

1. Build connections	1.
2. Set boundaries	2.
3. Open to change	3.
4. Manage discomfort	4.
5. Choose goals	5.
6. Identify options	6.
7. Take action	7.
8. Persevere (keep trying)	8.

Look at your "Most Useful" list and glance back at your "Hardest to Easiest" list. Where do you want to start? Where could you use more support right now?

Make a plan

There are dozens of strengthening exercises in this book. What's the best order for you? Print out or dog ear (fold over the corner so you can find it easily) the list on the next page, because you're going to customize your own Resilience Plan. Based on the lists you've made above, and what you know about your challenges right now, ask yourself: "In what order do I want to learn these skills?

You'll fill in each skill—in the order that works best for you—on the "Section" line, until you've got them all.

Then, since you've already accomplished the whole introduction, you can check off the first eight boxes under "Introduction"!

Two More Very Important Things

1. For the exercises to work, you have to actually do them, not just skim or read them. I get it—you're busy. However, you know how reading about an exercise plan doesn't give the benefits of actually lifting the weights? This is definitely one of those annoying situations in which you have to do the work. You'll benefit a ton if you do.

2. **You're not alone!** People all over the world have become more aware than ever of the need for resilience. They want to encourage you, and I want to support you. So every time you finish a section, go to the link and share a little about the skill you just built. And you'll get a different prize at the end of each section!

MY RESILIENCE PLAN

☐ **Introduction**
    ☐ Chapter 1—We Believe a Lie
    ☐ Chapter 2—So What's the Truth?
    ☐ Chapter 3—All Change Is Stressful
    ☐ Chapter 4—Why Our Brains Hate Change
    ☐ Chapter 5—What Is the Answer to All This Struggle?
    ☐ Chapter 6—Learn Resilience on Purpose
    ☐ Chapter 7—The Ingredients of Resilience
    ☐ Chapter 8—How to Use This Book

☐ **Section** _____
    ☐ Exercise _____
    ☐ Exercise _____
    ☐ Exercise _____
    ☐ Exercise _____
    ☐ Get online and report back!

☐ **Section** _____
    ☐ Exercise _____
    ☐ Exercise _____
    ☐ Exercise _____
    ☐ Exercise _____
    ☐ Get online and report back!

☐ **Section** _____
    ☐ Exercise _____

- ☐ Exercise _____
- ☐ Exercise _____
- ☐ Exercise _____
- ☐ Get online and report back!

☐ **Section** _____

- ☐ Exercise _____
- ☐ Exercise _____
- ☐ Exercise _____
- ☐ Exercise _____
- ☐ Get online and report back!

☐ **Section** _____

- ☐ Exercise _____
- ☐ Exercise _____
- ☐ Exercise _____
- ☐ Exercise _____
- ☐ Get online and report back!

☐ **Section** _____

- ☐ Exercise _____
- ☐ Exercise _____
- ☐ Exercise _____
- ☐ Exercise _____
- ☐ Get online and report back!

☐ **Section** _____

- ☐ Exercise _____
- ☐ Exercise _____
- ☐ Exercise _____
- ☐ Exercise _____
- ☐ Get online and report back!

☐ **Section** _____

- ☐ Exercise _____
- ☐ Exercise _____
- ☐ Exercise _____
- ☐ Exercise _____
- ☐ Get online and report back!

☐ **Now What? (conclusion)**
- ☐ Integrity and Purpose
- ☐ How 'Bout Them Attributes!
- ☐ Seriously, Congratulations
• I'll miss you! Unless . . .

AMPLIFY YOUR WORK

YOU'VE BEATEN THE ODDS. Not only did you *open* a book that could make you stronger, you've read the introduction (often the most boring part).

Make It Work for You

Most research on mental health and self-development shows that the benefits of reading and thinking about these concepts decrease quickly after you close the book unless you connect to the work in other aspects of your life.

SO! Please follow this QR code by focusing your camera app on this code with your phone or tablet and clicking on the website that comes up.

Why would you do that?

For all these reasons:

1. Waiting for you at the end of each section is a **different free gift** specific to that resilience skill.
2. You'll grab a badge for each skill and be able to track your progress.
3. You will be more successful at building your resilience if you connect to other people who are doing the same. Check it out. You'll see what I mean!

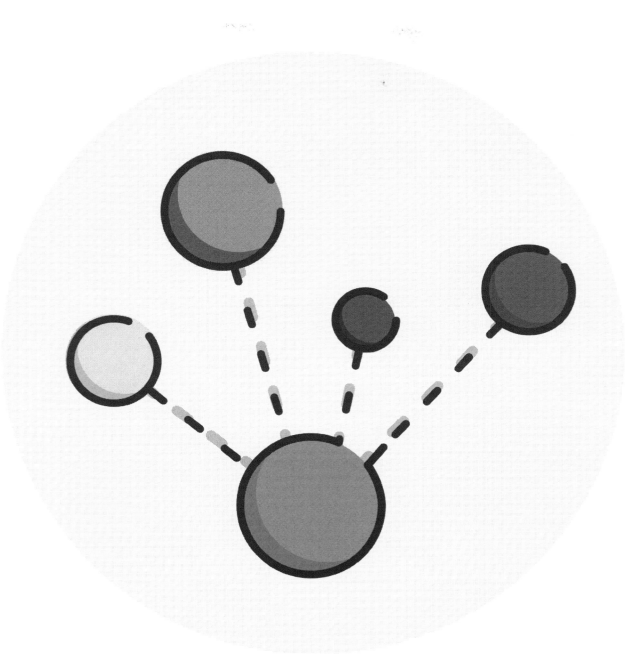

Build Connections

BUILD
CONNECTIONS

AT A WORK CONFERENCE IN ATLANTIC CITY, I got a push notification on my phone from United Airlines. "Your flight FCO -> JFK has been delayed to 1300 tomorrow." FCO, that's Rome.

My son, my fifteen-year-old son, who had found a free year-abroad program to do for all of tenth grade, was due to fly home.

And 1300 (1pm) tomorrow? That would mean a twenty-two-hour layover in Rome. Overnight. Did I mention he was fifteen??

I called the airline.

"Sì, signora, all is well! We will give your son the voucher. With this he can stay at any of the hotels close to the airport."

I explained that my son was fifteen and in my experience hotels would not allow kids to check in alone. He agreed that was probably true and that he was very sorry, but he could not help me further.

My son was already on his first flight, about to land in a city where neither of us knew anyone, he didn't speak the language, and he had nowhere to stay overnight. This trip, which had seemed reasonable (and was the least expensive option) when we booked it, now seemed like a huge parenting mistake.

I was scared! I could picture him trying to sleep on the chairs at a gate in the airport while keeping track of his stuff. I could picture security telling him he couldn't stay overnight in the airport and then him outside in the dark . . .

We needed a person. I didn't know who, but I knew we needed someone in Rome to connect to who would care about my son's situation and help him find a safe place to stay and a way to get there and back to the airport.

I didn't have the connections I needed, but I remembered something that I've learned over the years:

You don't even know everyone you know.

It was time to ask the connections I did have about the connections they had and see who we could meet. So I put out the word. Boy, did I ever.

I started with a Facebook post:

I knew that I needed to widen my connections to solve this problem, and quickly. I needed to find trustworthy people, people who had compassion and would be good problem-solvers. Often the best way to widen your network of connections is by going to and through the connections you already have.

Comments and messages and then texts started to come in, and sure enough, I knew someone whose niece was a medical student living in Rome. She had a couch, and he could sleep on it if he'd like. She had a test, though, and no car, so she couldn't collect him from the airport.

Someone else had a contact at a religious organization that regularly met refugees at the airport. They'd meet my son and drop him off if needed.

Arrangements made, I had to face the next hurdle: how to communicate all these changes to my son. At the time he would land, I had to be onstage, busy for an hour giving a seminar at the conference, and would not be able to troubleshoot or answer his questions. He needed to understand what was happening and go meet the organization's driver—who didn't speak English—and make his way to this medical student's apartment. Since we hadn't thought to get him a European SIM card for his phone, he would only be able to use his phone while he had Wi-Fi at the airport or after he got to her apartment.

I needed someone to babysit my phone and answer my son when he reached out. Someone who could understand the situation and communicate clearly to him what he needed to do, without totally freaking him out. Bonus if they wouldn't judge me too hard for allowing my fifteen-year-old to travel internationally alone!

The conference was full of great people, but no one I felt I knew well enough to ask for this kind of favor. Well, it was time to fix that!

I had to choose a connection to deepen. Asking for help is a huge obstacle for me, but what's embarrassment and discomfort compared to my son's safety, right? OK, it's a lot, but I couldn't see another option. I went to a woman I thought might understand and also say yes. I took a deep breath and then just laid out the situation to her, mom to mom.

She was happy to help!

When I stepped offstage, I dove straight for her. "He's thrilled!" she reported. "He met up with the guy picking up the refugees, and he's on his way to the med student's apartment. He's talking about going out to take some pictures and eat gelato. He'll text you when he gets to her place."

Building connections is one of the first skills we learn as children. Kids learn fast that, when they want something, they often need other people to help them. They need people who are taller (to reach the cookies), stronger (to open the cookies), and have a car (to buy the cookies). Just for example.

The same is true of adults. The wider and deeper your support network, the more resilient you can be when you face a change or a problem.

That phrase, though, "support network," can be intimidating, right? It's one thing to think of all the people you *know*. It's much harder to think of who you'd be willing to *ask for help*.

A support network isn't all about asking favors or leaning on people. It's about having a large number of folks to choose from when you have a question. The goal is to know more people so that you can ask the *right* person your question or your favor.

I've got some bad news though.

Knowing people isn't enough. Just having a large number of friends on your social media profile or a long email contact list or even a fat address book doesn't mean you have connections. In order to form a connection, you have to have an exchange with that person.

Exchange ideas. Share a smile or a laugh or a knowing look at a work meeting. Offer a suggestion, lend a hand, offer quiet support for that person. Give an honest answer when they ask how you are. Ask a follow-up question instead of just being polite. Hold a door, help carry a couch, offer to lend a hand with a project. Watch something they like, share music, ask them to read something you learned from or something you wrote.

This section is all about things you can do right now to build connections wider or deeper, so that your network is there when you need it and you can find the right person when you have need and be the right person for someone else when they do.

HELP WANTED

PURPOSE: Build connections wider.

Consider what kinds of problems you'd like help solving. Do you need someone to just listen to what's bothering you? Do you want IT (technology) support? Do you often have questions about house repair? Are you often longing for someone to give you perspective on your relationship or your job? Would it be great to have a person to guide you in your parenting decisions?

Do you wish you had someone who listened without telling you what to do? Or would you prefer someone who gave advice that was easy to follow? When do you feel comfortable asking for help and when do you feel like you're a burden on the person you're asking?

Finding the right kind of help can be hard. This exercise is going to make it easier!

Pick one kind of connection you'd like to build. Follow these steps to create an ad for that new person in your support network. Are you going to post it online? Nope. The goal here is to figure out who you are really looking for, and then we'll talk about where you can find them.

Who Is Searching?

First, let's figure out a little about you.

What are some words to describe you? List a few true, positive adjectives about yourself, words you think a person who knows you well and really likes you would use to describe you. (Be honest! It's not bragging.)

_____

_____

_____

What needs do you have right now? What problems or rough spots are you facing? What do you feel is missing right now?

_____

_____

_____

Where do you want a new or deeper connection to fit in your life? Will this be an Internet friend? Someone you see around in your community? Someone you can text twice (or twenty times) a day?

_____

_____

_____

Who Do You Need?

Who are you looking for? In what part of your life are you looking to expand your connections? Do you need someone at work or someone who understands your job? Someone who lives in a similar situation to you? Someone who "speaks your language" about a hobby or interest or past experience? Someone with a lot of knowledge in a particular area? What are some requirements for this person?

_____

_____

_____

How do you feel most supported? Are you looking for someone who is a great listener? Who will validate your choices? Who knows more than you do? Who gives lots of empathy? Someone who can motivate you? Do you want someone who tells the truth even when you don't want to hear it?

_____

_____

_____

What doesn't work for you? When you have a conversation with a friend or a connection, what do you wish they wouldn't do? What doesn't feel like help to you? What frustrates or angers you when someone gives advice or listens to a struggle?

_____

_____

_____

Now Let's Put It Together.

Go back to your answers to fill in these blanks—the () underneath each section below corresponds to the questions above. Pull the most important parts for your answers.

Your classified ad here:

_____

(What are some words to describe you?)

Person ISO (in search of) wider network to

_____

_____

_____

(What need do you hope this person will meet?)

Applicant should be familiar with

_____

_____

_____

(Who are you looking for?)

and able to easily

_____

_____

_____

(How do you feel most supported?)

but not

_____

_____

_____

(What doesn't work for you?)

Person should be ready to

_____

_____

_____

(Where do you want this connection to fit in your life?)

Now What?

Read through your Help Wanted ad (I'm not asking you to post this anywhere!).

Think about where you might meet this person. Where wouldn't you meet this person? Have you been trying to get some people in your life to fill this "job" who just aren't the right people? The purpose of this activity is to help you understand who you'd like to find. You can do this as often as you'd like to figure out who you want to get to know in different parts of your life.

Just by deciding who you want to know, you are becoming more resilient!

Knowing what you're looking for in your support network makes you much more likely to find it.

Other activities in this section will help you figure out how to create new connections, how to deepen connections to people you already know, and how to know who you don't want to be connected with after all.

WHO'S YOUR ICE? (IN CASE OF EMERGENCY)

PURPOSE: Build connections deeper.

Imagine your day goes totally sideways. Your car breaks down or somebody at work quits. You lose something important or someone you care about gets sick. Who do you call?

Most of us have a few go-to humans whom we reach out to when things are hard. Often, though, those interactions don't help as much as you wished they did, or they actually make your day worse.

This exercise will help you figure out who to call when you can't solve a problem alone.

Help Tracker

Resilience requires asking for help. Asking is hard, and often it isn't enough! You also have to figure out who to ask—which totally depends, right? It can depend on what you need, how fast you need it, and even the time of day that you need help. This log is to help you document what—or who—you've tried so far, so you'll know who to reach out to and what to ask in the future.

When have you needed help? In the past few days, weeks, or months, what problems have come up that you needed help to solve? Pick three that you can remember. They can be big or small.

Problem #1 _____

Problem #2 _____

Problem #3 _____

Who did you call? Try to remember each person you asked in the situation and who answered.

Problem #1 _____

Problem #2 _____

Problem #3 _____

How did it go? "Just ask for help." Sounds simple and almost never is. So, when you asked for help, what happened? Did the problem get solved? Did you feel supported or indebted to that person? Did your day get easier or harder? What was useful and what was frustrating?

Problem #1
Positive Outcomes:

_____

_____

_____

Negative Outcomes:

_____

_____

_____

Problem #2
Positive Outcomes:

_____

_____

_____

Negative Outcomes:

_____

_____

_____

Problem #3
Positive Outcomes:

_____

_____

_____

Negative Outcomes:

_____

_____

_____

The purpose here is not to decide who is a good friend or a good person. Most people really want to help and do the very best they can. The purpose is to figure out who truly understands how to help you and has the particular skills or personality to match well with yours when you're in need.

Who helped you build resilience—navigate change and come through it with integrity and purpose—and who didn't? Did any of these situations get harder when you asked that person for help?

Why does this matter?

When we build connections, we create patterns. There are people who regularly come to you for help and yet you hesitate or don't even think to ask them when you need a hand. You also probably have people you ask for help because you feel you "should" based on their role in your life or because they'd be hurt if you didn't.

Resilience requires building connections that are useful and actually make life easier.

No one else needs to see what you've written here or know what you're thinking. The goal of this exercise is for you to have more success when you reach out for help. Keeping the last couple of pages in mind, who is your "ICE" (In Case of Emergency) person for each of these situations?

PERSON   **TYPE OF PROBLEM**

_____   Car/Transportation Issues

_____   Work Problems

_____ Career Guidance

_____ Health Worries

_____ Relationship Problems

_____ Need a Great Listener

_____ Family Advice

_____ True Emergency

_____ _____ (fill this in)

_____ _____ (fill this in)

_____ _____ (fill this in)

Now What?

Consider this list the next time you need a hand. Whether your go-to person is available or not isn't so important. What matters is that you ask for help from someone who has the knowledge and the ability to give you the kind of help you really need. Oh, and put that True Emergency person in your phone contacts under "ICE." That's who the police or hospital will call if you're not able to answer questions for yourself. Just a little friendly PSA from your neighborhood family physician.

CAST A WIDER NET(WORK)

PURPOSE: Build connections wider.

Do you have a friend wish list? People you've met or seen or read about whom you just know you would get along great with?

No, this is not a guide to becoming a stalker.

This is a guide to Connecting with New People.

The more people you know, the more likely you are to have the network of support that you need when you need it.

There are times in life that are easier for making new connections. You'll meet a lot of people who are open to new bonds if you are all together at the beginning of something: the beginning of an educational opportunity like a training program, the beginning of a committee or organization, the beginning of an event that is for the purpose of creating those bonds, like a networking conference or a mentorship program. Another advantage to these situations is that you're surrounded by people with whom you have at least one thing in common, and you just need to pick from that group.

The more adult or established we get, though, the less often those "we're all new here" opportunities occur. So you need to learn how to pick people you want to connect to *and* figure out how to get to know them. That's where this exercise will help you.

Connections Wish List

In addition to the people you have in your life, who else would you like to know? Let's divide your world into categories. Think about the people in these groups and write down the names (or description, if you don't know their first name) of some folks you might like to get to know.

Work   Neighborhood/Community   Family Events

_____

_____

_____

Exercise/Gym   Places You Volunteer   House of Worship

_____

_____

_____

Group or Club   Adults at Places You Take Kids   Coffee Shop, etc.

_____

_____

_____

And one more. What celebrity would you like to know better? I don't mean someone who has an entourage, or a bodyguard, or a Secret Service agent. I mean, is there a local musician or athlete or blogger or podcast host or someone else who is a little famous whom you really appreciate? Aiming outside your usual social circles for someone you admire is often surprisingly successful, and those connections can offer new perspectives on your own pursuits.

Courting a New Connection

"Courting" is a truly old-fashioned word that means to seek someone's attention and affection. How can you get the attention of one of the people you've listed and help them want to connect with you? First of all, pick the three people from the lists you've made whom you'd really like to get to know.

1. _____

2. _____

3. _____

Now answer these questions about each of them:

What We Have in Common   Why I Want to Connect

1. _____   _____

2. _____   _____

3. _____   _____

Reaching Out

Finding a reason to interact with someone isn't complicated. Pick something that will add a little value or joy to their life and then offer a follow-up. Sounds like business networking, right? This is the same principle and works for the same reason.

Most people reach out for the first time to ask a favor or add to someone's list of things they have to do. That leads to a negative chemical reaction in the brain. You are going to avoid that pathway by reaching out in a way that makes someone feel good.

Below is a list of ways to relate to someone new. Circle all the options that feel possible for you to actually do.

1. Notice (out loud or in a message) something good they did or do.
2. Ask a question about something they said they enjoy.
3. Admire how they did something.
4. Ask their opinion on something related to your common interest.
5. Share something funny related to your common experience.
6. Offer assistance if they've expressed a desire for help.
7. Do a kindness. For example, ask if they'd like something when you're getting up.
8. Share a resource or thought-provoking article.
9. _____ (something else you've thought of)

Match the Strategy to the Person

What do you think might work best with which person? OK, that might be a little confusing. Just fill this out:

Name	Why I Want to Connect	Possible Strategies (list #'s from list above)
Example: *Gwynn from work*	*She handles our boss!*	*#1, #2, #4, #7*
1._____	_____	_____
2._____	_____	_____
3._____	_____	_____

Actually Connect

You've named a few people you'd like to reach. You've thought about why and how. You've outlined a plan. Now it's time to follow through.

First, go to the "Possible Strategies" you listed above and circle the strategy that seems most likely to be successful for each of those people.

Now make your plan. Think about the strategy you'll try first and when you'll try it. Consider what you'd like to do after you make that connection. Do you want to get together? Do you just want to be more comfortable asking a question at some later date? Will you send another thoughtful message in a while?

Name	Strategy	I'll Do This On	Follow Up
Gwynn from work	*#2*	*Next Monday*	*Email for coffee plans*
1._____	_____	_____	_____
2._____	_____	_____	_____
3._____	_____	_____	_____

Now What?

Put these in your calendar or set an alarm in your phone. Reaching out to these people will strengthen your resilience. Whether or not any of these folks become your new best friend is not important. You are learning to widen your network and connect to more people. That skill will make you more resilient.

CURIOSITY. KINDNESS. GRATITUDE.

PURPOSE: Build connections deeper.

"You don't even know what you don't know about the people in your life."

A high school teacher said this to my eleventh-grade English class at the beginning of our unit on journalism. He'd assigned us interviews and told us to start with the people we thought we knew well. "They do things, think things, know things that you've never even considered," he went on. "And that can benefit you. Go find out how."

Have you ever been talking to someone in your life about a way you were stuck, and that person surprised you with a great solution? Or did you ever run into someone you knew from work at an event for a group you belong to? Have you been shocked to learn that friends of yours knew each other some other way, like through an activity that you had no idea they even did? Most of us can count on one hand the people we know most everything about.

Knowing more about the people in your life is incredibly valuable. Why? Because, when you're connected to someone, their skills, their knowledge, and the people *they* know and are connected to all become more accessible to you.

I'm in a Facebook group for women who are moms and physicians. I know it sounds niche, but there are over eighty thousand people in this group, and requests for help—for ourselves, our families, and our patients—are a daily occurrence. Many of these requests are wildly specific, like "Does anyone know quarterback Tom Brady? I have a patient whose dying wish is to speak to him," "Is anyone a pediatric neurologist at the Columbia Asia International Clinic in Saigon? My niece is there and needs help," and "Has anyone experienced a weird noise in their Honda Odyssey after taking out the center seat? What *is* that?"

Most likely, though, you don't have access to eighty thousand engaged strangers, so you need to get to know the connections you do have a little better. You could absolutely interview each person in your life for a journalism project (it was a very cool project), if you have time. In the meantime, there are other ways to get to know your people better.

Deepening your connections involves strengthening your bonds to those people. Knowing who you know is useful. Reminding yourself and them of the importance of your relationship is crucial.

Curiosity—Investigate Your People

It's easy to make assumptions about friends and family, that you know what they do and what their interests are and what they're good at in their lives. It's time to get curious! You don't even know what you don't know about them.

Who do you want to know better? Pick a question below, then text or call or sit down with them and ask. And write down their answer below.

- About what subject are you kind of an expert?
- What's something you're excellent at doing?
- If you had two hundred dollars to spend on a hobby, what would you pick?
- Who's the most interesting person you know well? Why?
- Where did you grow up? Do you keep in touch with people there?
- What task or role are you best at in your job?
- What is the coolest group you've ever belonged to?
- What's the farthest you've ever lived from where we are now?
- Who is the most famous or powerful person you know?
- What is your superpower?
- If you lived two hundred years ago, what job would you have?
- What's something you know that you wish you could teach everyone?
- Who is your role model?
- What don't I know about you that I really should?
- _____ (you fill it in)

Who Will You Ask?   Which Question?

_____   _____

Their Answer:

_____

_____

_____

Who Will You Ask?   Which Question?

_____   _____

Their Answer:

_____

_____

_____

Who Will You Ask?   Which Question?

_____   _____

Their Answer:

_____

_____

_____

Kindness—Support Your People

Do your people know that they matter to you? If you answered "of course!" that's great . . . but I want you to stop for a moment and be really sure. "Of course" is not always for sure, even when we think it is.

Robert Waldinger, a psychiatrist and professor at Harvard Medical School, gave an interview to the Harvard Gazette in 2017. He explained that the Harvard Study of Adult Development—one of the world's longest ongoing studies of adult life, started in 1938—showed that "People who fared the best were the people who leaned into relationships, with family, with friends, with community." Making sure that your people know they matter to you doesn't just strengthen those relationships, it strengthens your resilience and your health.

Active kindness builds those bonds. Active kindness means finding something—a cup of coffee, a quick text to ask how someone is doing, a supportive look or word during a difficult experience—that positively shows someone you get them. And that you're willing to take the time to show them. Make a list and follow through.

Who Will You Show?   Kind Act:

_____   _____ ☐ Done

_____   _____ ☐ Done

_____   _____ ☐ Done

Gratitude—Tell Your People

The relational and health benefits of expressing gratitude are well researched and documented. Expressing gratitude is not the same as a kind act. As a matter of fact, it's even easier! You just need to do two things.

1. **Notice something a person does.** I don't mean something they have or are or were born with but a choice they made or an action they took. Gratitude in this case means expressing appreciation for something someone else did intentionally. When you are explicitly thankful for something that person can control, they feel a stronger sense of accomplishment and a deeper connection to you.

2. **Express your gratitude clearly and without any strings attached.** This is not the moment to ask a favor or offer a critique. Standalone gratitude is the way to make sure that other person knows that they have impacted you for the good. Mix that with any other message—like "could you drop off that sweater you said I could borrow" or even "hope the weather is great"—and you take away from the power of your message.

Who Will You Tell?   What Do You Appreciate?

_____ ☐ Done

_____ ☐ Done

_____ ☐ Done

Now What?

Try one from each list today. Today! Actually. You'll see really incredible results. As a matter of fact, this may be so gratifying that you decide to make a longer list. These kinds of outreaches will mean more to your people than you could possibly know, until someone turns around and does this for you.

YOU DID THAT!

CONGRATULATIONS! You strengthened your resilience by building connections.

I have one more idea for you. Think about someone you depend on when you're in a tough spot.

Who is it? _____

Right now—while you're *not* in a tough spot—reach out to them to tell them you value, love, or otherwise appreciate them.

Now for the Best Part

I want to celebrate you! Please follow this QR code by focusing your camera app on this code with your phone or tablet and clicking on the website that comes up.

Why would you do this?

Three reasons!

1. You can answer the question there about your experience building connections and see what other people have noticed—come grow your connections!
2. Get your badge!
3. **There's a gift** to aid you in building connections with ninety-seven ways to show your appreciation for someone in your life— and most of them are free!

Set Boundaries

SET
BOUNDARIES

"EVERY TIME YOU SAY 'YES' TO SOMETHING, you're saying 'no' to something else."

Boom.

Do you remember the cartoons in which the character is walking down the road and a piano drops on their head? That statement hit me exactly like a grand piano pushed out a third-story window above a busy city street. Tory Johnson, the keynote speaker at a conference I was attending said this one sentence; it quite literally changed my life.

I had spent the majority of my adulthood saying yes to everybody. Every time someone asked me to pitch in, volunteer, do something extra, I said yes. And because I'm a loud person who goes to things, I was often asked.

As a mom of four kids who were four, six, eight, and ten at the time, I was helping with preschool, kindergarten, and third- and fifth-grade stuff: soccer team(s) parent, travel carpool, community service projects, teacher appreciation week, parent association board. Also, you know, loving and raising and listening to and mediating between the kids themselves, right?

As a doctor, I was seeing patients in the office, teaching and evaluating medical students, was on call 24/7 every other week for a week at a time, performed rounds on patients at the hospital, made house calls (yup), appealed to insurance companies on behalf of my patients for needed tests or procedures or medicine, answered patient emails and calls before and after office hours, read and tested and learned to meet Continuing Medical Education requirements, and went to medical staff and department meetings.

As the main organizer at home, I planned and executed allthethings: grocery shopping, cooking meals, making sure everyone had clean clothes to wear that (mostly) fit, and arranging schedules and car repair and household chores.

And I was the go-to person when things went sideways, when a kid got sick or one of my parents did, when something broke or was lost or a schedule changed, or when a colleague needed coverage.

This was the summer of 2012 and I had just been asked to host a new TV show for my local PBS station. Oh boy, I wanted to say yes. The show was about technology and its impact on families. As a doctor and as a mom, I could see the tremendous issue this was becoming. Here was a chance to help lots of families get answers to problems we were facing every day.

There was no way I could do it though. I mean, *how* would I have time?

Then I went to that conference where the keynote speaker taught me an entire semester's worth of self-management in that one sentence:

"Every time you say 'yes' to something, you're saying 'no' to something else."

Think about that for yourself. When you say yes to a new project at work, you're saying no to spending as many hours as you are now on the projects you already have. Maybe that's great because you have the time and you want the opportunity   . Maybe you'll get a chance to shine and advance, earn more, feel more fulfilled at work. Or maybe that means you won't perform as well with your current responsibilities. Maybe you'll get frustrated and irritable. Maybe you'll stay longer at work and pull from other parts of your life.

When you say yes to planning your friend's birthday, you're saying no to something else you planned to do with your free time. Maybe that's great because you've been wanting to spend time with this person and their friends—you miss them and it will feel excellent to reconnect. Or maybe this means you'll postpone (again) your new plan to exercise after work. Or you'll get less sleep, or you won't have time to watch the show you're binging with your partner.

For me, the PBS opportunity meant investigating all those tasks that had me so very busy. Did each of them really have to get done at all, and did each of them have to get done by me? I learned I was doing a lot that I could teach and delegate to my kids (that's a whole different set of books, which I hope you'll check out!) or let go of in favor of doing the things that mattered most and that only I could do. For myself, for my family, for my patients, for my community, I decided I could let the laundry go a bit and teach my boys to fold their own (just for example) if it meant I could say yes to the project at WQED on families and technology.

The trick is to recognize the benefits *and the cost* of saying yes and then make a decision.

We need to talk about three things to really understand why we don't do this and how we could.

1. Saying no is a privilege. Most people don't get a lot of choice about what they say yes or no to in the grand scheme of things. We need to work because we need money. We have kids and parents and other people to take care of because we love them and they need us. We have groceries to buy and people to clothe, and all of that is fact. So finding the opportunities when you could say no—the ones outside those requirements—can be really hard to spot.

2. Saying no is hard. It feels great to say yes. More than that, many of us connect our self-worth to making others happy. Disappointing someone—anyone but ourselves—can be a huge obstacle. We'd much rather disappoint or even damage ourselves than make anyone else at all uncomfortable.

3. Saying no is crucial to resilience. Have you heard the expression "You can't be all things to all people"? Well, you absolutely can, but not for long. Saying yes to everyone else will not leave you the strength or resources you need to get the life you want.

Living life without boundaries drains your time and your energy and your joy. The purpose of resilience is to navigate through life able to achieve your goals. Set boundaries around your time and energy so that the choices you make move you forward instead of keeping you stuck.

So How Are You Supposed to Know When to Say No?

The following exercises will help you define your priorities. Once you're rock solid clear on your priorities, you'll be able to see how to match your commitments to those goals. You'll practice the skill of setting boundaries and see the value it has in your life.

WHAT MATTERS?

PURPOSE: To define your priorities.

I heard Oprah on a podcast tell a story about a guest she had on her morning TV show a couple of decades ago (retold in my words here). This guest asked her audience to take the beautiful pen and notebook that had been placed underneath each audience member's seat. (You get a pen. And you get a pen! And *you* get a pen!)

"Please write down your top five priorities in life. Who or what is most important for you to take care of in your life?"

Try that, would you?

Who or what is most important for you to take care of in your life?

1. _____

2. _____

3. _____

4. _____

5. _____

The guest then asked the audience to raise their hand if they'd put themselves on the list. Not a single hand went up.

"You should be on the list!" this woman exclaimed. "You belong at the *top* of your list!"

Oprah stood next to her, nodding and smiling, when the audience started to grumble. The grumbles were followed by a few shouts of "No!" and the audience began to boo.

Oprah was horrified. According to her retelling on the the NPR podcast mini-seires "Making Oprah," she spoke directly to her audience and said, "What is happening right now? This woman is a guest in my house. We don't boo a guest in my house!" Then, she explained, she needed to know why the audience was so angry. "What is wrong? She didn't tell you to divorce your husbands! She didn't tell you to leave your kids or your parents starving in the street! She said *you* should be someone you take care of!"

This was an epiphany for Oprah—that's why she was talking about it on a podcast. She realized that adults had been told—especially women—that our job is to care for others, that our worth is entirely dependent on our value to others, even if it means harming ourselves.

Does this sound true in your life?

What do you spend time doing? Make a list—really think about your days. Look through your calendar, your text messages, your to-do list, and your work email, and write down the tasks you did in the last week or so.

_____   _____

_____   _____

_____   _____

_____   _____

Now, grab a highlighter or a pen of a different color. Go back through that list and circle all the ones that match your top five priorities. For example, if you have "my family" on the priority list, you'll circle any family members on this list and also anything you did to help a family member, like grocery shopping. If you have "my health" on that Top Five Priorities list, you should circle "exercise" or "doctor's appointment" on this list. If you don't know whether to circle something or not, ask yourself, "Why did I do that? Who did it help?" That should help you decide if it supported one of your priorities.

What didn't you have time for in the last week that you wanted to do? Are there tasks or fun things or meaningful experiences that you thought about recently but couldn't fit into your schedule?

_____   _____

_____   _____

_____   _____

_____   _____

Grab that highlighter or pen and circle the ones that align with your Top Five Priorities.

Now What?

We absolutely can't say no to everything we don't feel like doing. But every time you say yes to something on that long list of tasks, you're saying no to something on the "want to do" list. Just something to consider.

WHAT'S THE POINT?

PURPOSE: To understand the roles that different things and people play in your life and to know when they're not meeting your needs.

Would you buy the best winter jacket you ever saw? It's your favorite color for clothing. It's made of your favorite material. It's completely affordable for you. You even *need* a new winter jacket. But they don't make it in your size or the size just above or below yours. Would you buy it?

Nope.

You'd want to. You'd ask if you could order it online or if the store could get it made in your size. You'd think about it later, maybe even search for it at other stores. But if it really doesn't fit, it doesn't matter how much you love it—it's not for you.

If it really doesn't fit, it doesn't matter how much you love it. It's not for you.

What do you want from your shoes? Seriously. What do you want—not just need—from a pair of shoes? Check off any and all of the reasons below that you have for buying and keeping a pair of shoes.

Good quality	Affordable	You like them	Good support
Comfortable	In style	Great for the weather	Look great
Good memories	Fit well	_____	_____

Now look at your checkmarks. Those are what you want in a shoe.

What do you need from your shoes?

Go back to that list and circle the thing or things you **have to have** in every pair of shoes you keep.

Now it's time to go to your shoe closet.

Grab an empty grocery or garbage bag because you may have a Goodwill donation to make. Bring your list along. You probably don't have to look through your shoes by the door—you wear those regularly so they probably meet your criteria. Go on over to the spot where you store the shoes you don't wear every day.

Look at your list and then look at each pair of shoes. Do they meet your **have to have** criteria? Great. Then if they meet any of your **want to have** criteria, keep them. Do you have any shoes that don't meet your needs? Even if they meet five of your wants, do they also meet your *needs*? If you have some shoes that just don't, it's time to free up a little space. Put them in the donation bag.

Did you find any shoes that aren't doing their job? _____

What about people?

You quite possibly saw this next part of the exercise coming. It's not only things that have a role in our lives. It's people too.

What's your favorite social media platform? Whether it's Facebook or Instagram or Tik Tok or email or your own little black book, this can be a great place to start thinking about what you want and what you need from your interactions there.

What do you want from your contacts?

Think about the purpose of the friends that you have or people that you follow on that platform. What do you want from them? Check off any and all of the reasons below that you have for connecting with and keeping a friend on that platform.

	Good support		They post useful info		They asked
	Friends in common		Professionally useful		Fun posts
	Honest/reliable		Interests in common		You like them
	Good memories		Aligned values		Respectful
	Know them in real life				

Now look at your checkmarks. Those are what you want in a friend in this space.

What do you need from your contacts?

Go back to that list and circle the thing or things you **have to have** in every one of your contacts on this platform.

Now it's time to go look at your "friends" list.

Take the time (and if you have a lot of contacts it might take a while) to go through your list. Make sure they fit your **have to have** criteria. All of them. As long as they do, keep them if you'd like. You can unfriend (yes, you can—it's your right and privilege to do so) anyone who doesn't meet your needs. You can even disconnect from the people who don't meet your wants, but that's less important.

The purpose here is to set some boundaries. If there are people showing up in your feed who don't meet your **have to have** list, they are dragging you down. They are sucking away some of your resilience. And it's your responsibility to do something about it.

Now What?

These are some bold moves I've suggested here. Throwing out shoes???

Seriously, it takes a lot of strength—and practice—to value yourself highly enough to walk away from what doesn't serve its purpose in your life. You may not feel ready to take this strategy into every aspect of your life. That's fine! The point here is to strengthen the skill of setting boundaries. **You** get to decide when to use that strategy.

GETTING RID OF YOUR BUT

PURPOSE: To see the potential in setting limits around your responsibilities.

What If You Could Shut It All Off and Just Do Something Great for You?

A big part of being resilient in the face of change and uncertainty is having the occasional break from change and uncertainty. That's right, taking a little time for yourself—whatever that means to you—can do more than recharge you. It actually heals your brain.

True mental breaks increase productivity, improve attention, and strengthen problem-solving.

What recharges you? Don't worry about how you'd make it happen, just list the activities that you do or want to do because they would help you feel great. Stay away from anything that costs too much money.

_____   _____

_____   _____

_____   _____

_____   _____

Which have you done this year? Go back to that list and put a checkmark by any that you've done in the past year. How did it affect you?

Activity   Outcome

_____   _____

_____   _____

_____   _____

_____   _____

_____   _____

_____   _____

When challenged to actually do something for themselves, most people say, "I'd like to, but . . ." **It's time to get rid of the but.**

I'll show you how.

Research studies of professionals who take time off list outcomes of increased energy, higher levels of happiness, and more resilience. They also list outcomes of feeling torn, more stress, and missed obligations.

What's the Problem?

Time. We believe we can't take the time.

So many surveys show that people—especially successful people—believe that the more we work, the more we'll succeed. And yet the research says the opposite. Google pushed their employees to commit to some time off (at least one day and one evening a week without any work, even checking in) and found that, when the employees actually did it, productivity went up![1]

As we keep talking about in this section, boundaries are about aligning what you do to your priorities. This is a further argument for making *you* a priority. But there's one huge obstacle most of us face when we think about taking time for ourselves.

Imagine you are away from home without access to the internet. You lose your phone. You are truly unreachable by others for an entire day and a night.

Even as you're problem-solving, right now in your head, how you could get to a phone or a phone store or back home . . . stop for a moment and ask a different question.

Who might need you? Did that question surprise you? Did you think I was going to ask about how peaceful it could feel or the advantages of being disconnected? Yeah, no. I want you to make a list of who you'd be worried about if no one could reach you. Think about work, family, friends. Consider who you genuinely feel responsible to at a moment's notice. Write down those names here:

_____   _____

_____   _____

_____   _____

_____   _____

Now, what if your disconnected time wasn't a surprise? What if you planned an afternoon or even a weekend with no way to reach you?

Who always needs to reach *you?*

Think about who has to be able to get hold of you in an emergency. Who are the reasons that you hesitate to turn your phone to silent? Who would you check on first thing after you got off an airplane with no Wi-Fi?

_____

_____

_____

Who Could Cover You?

In medicine, we spend a lot of our life on call. If I do the math, I've spent about 182 days a year (twenty-four hours a day each of those days) on call for my practice. That means I can be away from my phone no more than ten minutes at a time, day or night, for an entire week. Add to that, I have four kids, so I've had four people whose health and safety are top of my own priorities since May of 2002. I'm an entrepreneur in this business I created nine years ago, with clients all over the world. And I'm an only child of aging parents. I'm on call for a lot of people and many reasons.

You have lots of reasons to be on call yourself. You just listed them at the beginning of this exercise. Here's a trick from the medical field that can totally change the way you see—and meet—your responsibilities.

Since we do spend so much of our time on call, doctors have developed a lot of culture around covering each other on call.

I have learned to reach out for coverage when I'm sick (though I've also taken call from my own bed in the Emergency Department while getting IV fluids for morning sickness), when one of my kids is sick, when my mom was sick, when my travel got delayed, and even when I just forgot another obligation.

I've also learned to be flexible and compassionate when someone needs me to cover them. Second-grader is in the school play about dental care? Sure—go see her be a singing toothbrush. I'll see your ten a.m. patient. Loan officer at the bank moved your meeting to Saturday? I'll tell the answering service to page me. Need to drive your mom to chemo? OK.

Everyone is replaceable for a short period of time.

What does this mean for you? You need to figure out who can cover you.

It won't be the same person in every situation. Some people can be parent-you for a bit. Someone can be work-you. Someone can be adult-child-you. Let's figure out who those people are.

Who always needs to reach you? Write these down again. These are your "on-call" obligations.

1. _____

2. _____

3. _____

Who could be you? Think about what the people you just wrote down might need in an emergency. Is it transportation? Decision-making? Comfort or encouragement? Now write down two or three possible people to "take call" for you and do what you would do in that situation. So, if your first obligation was to your kids, who are a few people who could step in and parent them for a short time in an emergency? Write all those folks on the first line. Fill this in for each of your on-call obligations above.

1. _____

2. _____

3. _____

The scariest question of all:

Now What?

What are you going to do with all this?

Now that you see that you can get some "on-call coverage" and that working more is not going to help you work better . . .

Will you take care of you?

Go back to that list of activities that would heal you. Pick one and put it on your calendar for sometime in the next ten days.

Activity:_____ Date:_____ Time:_____ Who Will Cover You?_____

PLAY A GAME

PURPOSE: To set boundaries around difficult experiences.

Resilience is your ability to navigate change and come through it with integrity and purpose. Many changes are painful. Boundaries are necessary to heal from that pain.

Did you ever fall hard and scrape yourself? Those scrapes are usually on the palms of the hands and sometimes on the knees. They can hurt like fire because so many sensory nerves are rubbed raw and stay raw during the healing process.

If you clean the scrape well, it starts to heal. After a day or two, there's a scab, and it hurts a little less, unless you bump it. After a week or so, it's almost totally healed, no more pain, just the skin changes that show you where the injury was.

Unless you pick at the wound.

If you pick at it, the scab won't form properly or do its job. It will continue to hurt and likely become infected. It will take much longer to heal. In fact, it may worsen and infect the skin, even the tissue and muscles around the injury.

The same is true of difficult experiences. You have to figure out how to "clean them well" so they can start to heal. There are whole books on just that topic! When you navigate something difficult, make sure that you have the chance to air it out—talk about it with the right people—and wash it clean.

After that part is done comes the healing. And that's when you need good boundaries. If you keep picking at the pain, going over the difficulty again and again, it won't heal. Not only won't it heal, but the pain often spreads.

Just like with scrapes, stresses that have been properly treated need some protection and time without touching in order to heal.

It can be very difficult to put boundaries around a bad experience or loss. Grief is not linear, and it seeps into unexpected places, showing up when we least expect it. Noticing that is no kind of failure. Picking at it, though, can cause more harm.

So it's important to get practice processing struggles and then leaving them be for a while so they can scab over and heal. Luckily, there are lots of ways to learn this skill, and some of them are actually fun!

Play a Game

Have you ever watched a group of kids play four square or basketball (or any game with a ball and an "out of bounds" line)? When the ball is out, it's out. That person loses, or the play is over. If it's on the line, they'll argue it or take a do-over. If it's in, they keep playing. Boundaries allow us to figure out what is done and what's still in play. When you see a player who is still arguing about an out-of-bounds call while the game continues without her, you're probably seeing someone who will lose that game.

Find a person—preferably a kid you know well; they're the best at this—and ask them to play a game with you. Any of these will give you some practice discarding what's "out" or went badly and moving on. Put a checkmark by any you think would be fun and circle the one you actually played.

	Checkers		Basketball		Four square		Gaga
	Tic-tac-toe		Chess		Hot lava		Ping-pong
	Among Us		Ticket to ride		Darts		Any video game in which you have more than one life

Any of these quick-paced games encourage your resilience. They force you to put a boundary around a bad play or a losing turn and concentrate on what's ahead in order to succeed.

Put Boundaries Around Your Day

This is a different game, and it has an endless list of benefits. Sometime in the evening—at dinner if you eat with someone or on the phone with a friend or partner or adult child or in your own journal—play High, Low, High.

1. **High:** Tell about something great that day: something that pleased you or surprised you (in a good way) or gave you a break or an insight, something someone did for you or a good feeling you had doing something for someone else, a problem you solved or a snag you expected but didn't hit. Tell the story, answer any questions, and talk about it if you want to.

2. **Low:** Explain a struggle you had that day: a time you felt sad or frustrated or disappointed or embarrassed or angry, an experience that was not at all what you hoped or an interaction with someone who hurt you, an unmet expectation or a moment of lost hope. Tell the story and explain your feelings. Accept advice only if you want to—this doesn't have to be about solving a problem. It's a chance to describe what happened and how you felt.

3. **High:** Find another thing that was good today. Take a minute to let go of the hard feelings from your low and tell this story, allowing yourself to feel the good feelings again as you describe them.

This pattern will build your resilience in several ways. It allows you to put boundaries around the difficult experience, keeping it from seeping into everything you remember and feel. Even if some of those hard feelings persist, you're reminded that you can have good feelings as well.

You practice letting something hard heal a little without picking at it constantly.

Try it now. Think about the past twenty-four hours and tell me.

What was a high?

_____

_____

_____

What was a low?

_____

_____

_____

What was another high?

_____

_____

_____

Now What?

Your feelings are yours. There are no rules about what to feel or when. But, when you feel able, the skill of putting boundaries around something (or someone) difficult will build your resilience.

Make sure you've said and done what you need to for the struggle to get "aired out and washed clean"—meaning express your feelings, find the lesson, and get a professional to help you process it if that will help.

Then practice letting that experience end. Talk about it in the past tense. Take opportunities *not* to talk about it. Focus on what comes next. Those boundaries, and that practice, will make future struggles much easier to manage.

YOU DID THAT!

WAY TO GO! You strengthened your resilience by setting boundaries.

I have one more idea for you. Is there one thing on your to-do list that you really *don't* have to do? That you could delegate to someone else, put off for a week or two, or just not do?

What is it? _____

Great. Stop letting it take up brain space. It's not for you today.

Now for the Best Part

Let's celebrate this accomplishment! Please follow this QR code by focusing your camera app on this code with your phone or tablet and clicking on the website that comes up.

Why?

Three reasons!

1. You can name a boundary you highly recommend and see what other people have suggested.
2. Get your badge!
3. **There's a gift** for you to remind yourself when you don't have to worry about something because it's not inside your boundaries!

Open to Change

OPEN TO CHANGE

DOES OPEN-MINDEDNESS MATTER?

"He knows exactly what he wants and how to drive his team toward those goals." In answer to the question *What is this employee's greatest strength*, his CEO had written that glowing compliment.

I was reading this performance review as a part of my work with a client company regarding their performance and retention struggles. This organization, comprised of smart, motivated people, had been losing money and hemorrhaging staff for several months.

The CEO identified this manager's team as having the highest success potential and wanted me to start here to find the obstacles to achieving that success. Individual surveys and interviews indicated that the manager knew his people well—the team was made up of folks who were highly knowledgeable and motivated but were also experiencing increasing levels of frustration and helplessness. They had clear—if sometimes contradictory—ideas about how to navigate the changes they faced, but their suggestions were constantly shot down or ignored.

The manager in question had drive and vision without the ability to consider ideas other than his own for how to meet their goals.

What Isn't Open-Mindedness?

You can be nice,
You can be thoughtful,

You can be caring,
You can be neutral,
You can believe something that others don't,
You can listen to opposing views,
You can even be *right* without being open-minded.

An open mind requires searching for credible arguments against your point of view before making a decision.

Doesn't that sound awful? Or like a waste of time? Sometimes it absolutely is an exercise in futility. You do not need to hold yourself to that standard for every decision you make.

However . . .This skill can be a game changer when you're struggling.

When it became clear to me that my marriage was ending, that all the "let's wait for it to get better" and "I'll try anything" and counselling wasn't going to give us the future I'd always pictured, I really struggled. I couldn't see a way forward. I couldn't figure out what to do.

Even while I recognized that the marriage was over, I couldn't see any future possibilities other than the one I'd always been aiming and working toward.

I had to—and it was one of the hardest things I've ever done—change what I wanted.

Over to You

Resilience requires recognizing the possibility that your path *and* your destination might change.

Whether you are struggling to navigate a

- relationship change
- medical issue
- job loss
- financial hardship
- family member's struggle
- housing move

or any other big obstacle, your openness to change can make all the difference.

In the following exercises you'll figure out when it's the destination that should change and when it's just the strategies to get there that need an update. You'll strengthen your ability to consider more possibilities and when to discard them and stick to your original plan.

Opening to change doesn't mean scrapping your plan entirely. It means considering the possibility that there's something you haven't thought of yet and that it could be just as good—or better.

YOUR CHANGE TOLERANCE

PURPOSE: To gain insight into your perception of change and learn how you can help yourself navigate and open to change.

Think about some changes you've experienced in the past two years.

A Change You Wanted

What was a change that you hoped for, worked toward, prayed or wished for that actually happened? Some examples might be a new job, a promotion, a romantic partner, a baby, a new home . . . Write down a change you pursued and accomplished!

_____

_____

_____

Mark on this line how difficult it was to adapt to that change in your life once it happened:

....

| Very Easy | Easy | Hard | Very Hard |

A Change That Surprised You

What was a change that you didn't see coming at all? Some examples might be a flat tire, a pandemic, getting fired, an illness, or it could have been a new job, a promotion, a romantic partner, a baby . . . Write down an unexpected change.

_____

_____

_____

Mark on this line how difficult it was to adapt to that change in your life once it happened:

....

Very Easy   Easy   Hard   Very Hard

Looking for Your Trends

What is a change you've experienced that

1. You wanted and expected?

_____

_____

2. You didn't expect, but when it happened you were happy?

_____

_____

3. You didn't want, but when it happened it didn't surprise you?

_____

_____

4. You didn't want and you didn't expect?

_____

_____

Now take the numbers above (1, 2, 3, 4) and place each on this line.

....
Very Easy   Easy   Hard   Very Hard

What do you notice?
When you look at that, keep in mind that #1 is a change you wanted and expected, #2 a change you liked but hadn't expected, #3 a change you didn't want but expected, and #4 a change you didn't want _and_ didn't expect. What do you notice about how it was for you to adapt to each of those changes?

_____

_____

_____

Which is easier for you to adapt to: a change you wanted or a change you expected?

_____ Wanted   _____ Expected   _____ Neither   _____ Unclear

Preparation matters

For most people, an unwanted, unexpected change is the very hardest to navigate because it forces us to deal with a situation we don't like _and_ change our picture of our own possible future at the same time.

Two strategies will help!

1. **Picture different outcomes.** When you make a decision or encounter a new situation, consider what you hope will happen and also what else might happen. As you think about those less desirable outcomes, decide the first thing you would do if that happened.

   Example: You're planning a week-long family vacation and need to take time off from work to do it. You'll put in for the time off, but that might not be approved. Can you pick a couple of other weeks for backup? Also, you know the co-worker in your department who will cover you that week is thinking of leaving. If that happens, you know your boss might ask you to cancel your trip. How could you answer if that happens? Lastly, you know that there are a couple of work emergencies that could bring you back early. Can you make a plan for the rest of your family to stay even if you need to leave? Any of those changes would still be difficult to navigate but much less so than if you never considered them beforehand!

   Disclaimer! This is a tough skill to master because it can activate anxiety. If you are easily triggered, then work on this skill later in your resilience building journey.

2. **Tell a variety of future-stories.**
   People ask us our "plans" all the time.
   "How long will you keep working here?"
   "Got any plans for the summer?"
   "How are you spending the holidays?"
   "Doing anything for your birthday?"

Instead of having a set answer, try out a few different possibilities. That keeps your mind open to the possibility of change.

Talking about different possibilities decreases the amount of anger or loss you will feel if your plans have to change.

Now What?

Opening to the possibility of change is an ongoing exercise. It is human nature to get locked into one path that leads to the destination we want. It takes a bit of intentionality and practice to keep ourselves open to other paths and other destinations.

The rest of the exercises in this section will help you make that openness a habit.

BRING BACK THAT FEELING

PURPOSE: To build resilience by replacing cancelled events.

Plans change. Everyone who adulted through the pandemic has seen that plans change. Sometimes that's fine, occasionally it's great, but often it's a big disappointment or lost opportunity.

One way to build resilience is to learn how to replace an event or experience with purpose. Resilience is the ability to navigate change and come through it with integrity and purpose.

Most of the time, when plans we've made have to change, we see it as an obstacle. The client cancels a meeting or asks to move it from in-person to Zoom. Your good friend schedules their birthday celebration for a day you can't make it. Your vacation gets flooded by thunderstorms. There are lots of disappointments and frustrations in experiences like these.

There is also opportunity.

Opening to change allows you to connect your goals to your reality.

What's the Opportunity?

Every time you need a new plan, you have the chance to figure out what you really, actually want. Let's face it, we spend a lot of our lives on autopilot, going from one task or event to the next (with stops on the couch in between if we're lucky). When something gets cancelled or rained out, we have a block of time to **use for resilience.**

What Do You Need?

The first question to ask is, how can I best replace this? Sometimes the answer is "catch up on other stuff" or "hit the couch and relax!" Either of those is great if it's intentional, meaning you actually think about this opportunity and decide that is what serves you best.

Take a Minute for Empathy

Don't totally ignore your frustration or disappointment at the change. Have empathy for yourself and the other people affected. Whatever the feelings are, acknowledge them (even if you disagree with the feelings or think they're unnecessary).

Now . . .

Figure out what the missed opportunity was supposed to accomplish and then replace it with something else that meets that same goal.

We're going to do this exercise twice: once for work and once for home.

The Scenario:

You've been invited to an in-person interview for a job you really want, at their office. They've asked you to prepare a business problem and solution presentation, and you're ready! You've prepared, practiced, and perfected your demonstration.

You get a message the night before that they're still interested, but one of their leadership team is traveling so they need to do the interview by phone.

What do you feel? Take the time to acknowledge your own feelings and have some empathy for yourself.

I'm feeling_____!

That's all totally reasonable, and hard.

What were the advantages of being in-person rather than on the phone? List the things you thought could happen or feelings you could elicit in your interviewer doing this in person:

_____

_____

_____

How could you accomplish those reactions over the phone? This is the hard part. Your brain is resisting the change, focusing on loss and distrust and discomfort. Push through to figure out some choices. What could you send ahead, what video could you record on your phone, what materials could you provide, what story could you tell, what else is still an option to make the same impression given the new circumstances?

_____

_____

_____

And they may be even more impressed because they see your ability to adapt and succeed in the face of unexpected change!

Is there anything that is better because of the change? Again, even while feeling the loss and distrust and discomfort, can you see any advantages in the new situation?

_____

_____

_____

Now let's use this same exercise in a personal situation to see how opening to change can benefit you even more.

The Scenario: Your day off is really going to be a day *off*. You have the exact right amount of fun activities and total relaxation on your hammock planned and have let everyone know that you will not be available for errands, work stuff, or general busy-ness.

You wake up that morning so excited! The skies are dark, the wind is blowing, the rain starts pouring, and . . . the power goes out.

What do you feel? What's running through your mind?

I'm feeling... _____!

I totally get it. Argh!

Why did you make the plan you had? List what you wanted to get out of the day and the feelings you were looking forward to having at the end of it.

_____

_____

_____

How could you get those same feelings indoors with no electricity? It may seem impossible, but it isn't. Your phone probably still has some charge if you want to call a friend you'd love to move in with for the day. Your roommate's or your kid's laptop could be hotspotted by your phone if you need to figure out where there are still restaurants delivering food or indoor activities that might be open that you'd love. You probably have a flashlight somewhere if you want to read an actual book or search for gold under the basement flooring. What are some things you could do that would give you the feelings you wanted at the end of the day and are still possible in the new circumstances?

_____

_____

_____

Is there anything that is better because of the change? Even while you acknowledge the loss and distrust and discomfort, can you see any advantages in the new situation?

_____

_____

_____

When you're forced to be this intentional, really think it through, you could end up doing something you love, that you'd never have made time for without the storm.

Now What?

Every single time you have to pivot, change your vision, adapt to new circumstances, you build resilience.

Sometimes you build that resilience because you change goals. You might take time to relax and recharge, to strengthen connections with yourself or others because you have an unexpected break.

Sometimes, you really wanted to reach the goal you were aiming for with the original plan. In that case, follow this same algorithm of asking:

1. What do I feel?
2. What did I want to accomplish with the original plan?
3. How could I meet those same goals under the new circumstances?
4. What about this new situation might be even better?

WHAT IF?

PURPOSE: To question your assumptions about your plans in order to see more possibilities.

What if you dressed up nicer than you have to today?

What if you got to work a different way (walk, bus, get a ride, hot air balloon)?

What if you ate lunch with someone you're not sure you like?

What if you asked for a raise or asked a client to buy something new?

What if you had leftovers-in-pajamas-on-the-roof dinner?

Objections

As you read through that list, what objections popped into your head? Check them off below:

____ Why would I do *that*?	____ That's inconvenient.
____ That sounds awful.	____ I'd look ridiculous.
____ I don't want to.	____ Too uncomfortable.
____ Is that even safe?	

Possibilities

Now look at the list again. Imagine you decided to do one of those things today. What would you choose? What might be one of your reasons **for** doing that?

I'd choose: Because it might:

_____   _____

_____   _____

_____   _____

_____   _____

_____   _____

You don't have to do any of these things. Just considering the possibilities builds this skill. If you want to, though, pick one (or make up your own) and see what that change brings to you!

Big Picture Possibilities

There are many areas of life in which it's common to feel stuck. I hope you're not feeling that way in too many areas at once, but can you name two areas of your life in which you'd like to see some change?

Area 1: _____

Area 2: _____

What are the obstacles to solving those problems? Be as specific as you can.

Area 1 Obstacles: Area 2 Obstacles:

_____   _____

_____   _____

_____   _____

_____   _____

_____   _____

Now look at those lists of obstacles. What are the assumptions you're making? What *if* you were wrong about one of those obstacles? For example, are you assuming that making a change would hurt someone else too much? Are you assuming that you're not disciplined enough to make a change? Are you assuming that there is no one in your life who would help you? Is it *possible* that you are mistaken about any of those obstacles?

Go to that list of obstacles and put a "?" next to any that you could question—any that *might* not be true.

As with the "what if" questions at the beginning of this exercise, you don't have to do any of these things or make any of these changes to become more resilient. Just *considering* that you might be wrong about your obstacles, that you could make a significant difference in the future, strengthens your resilience. That way, when you're ready to make a change, you'll be more open to it.

Very Specific Possibilities

Have you been told you're a picky eater? If you have, you're actually a very *brave* eater! Me, I'm not a brave eater at all. It doesn't take any courage for me to try a new food because I like almost anything! I don't need to use any bravery when someone asks me to try something I haven't had before.

On the other hand, you (or any picky eater you know) have had a bunch of bad experiences with new tastes, so the act of trying another new thing takes a *lot* of courage. You know exactly how bad it can be, and it's hard to convince yourself to face that likely outcome, especially when you know a few foods that you really like. Why not just stick to those?

That act, though, of trying something new when you're pretty sure it will be unpleasant, that makes you more resilient. Opening yourself to the possibility that this next new food might be great builds the open-to-change skill.

Own Your Pickiness

What are you picky about? Check off anything on the list that you have strong opinions about and really don't like most things outside your favorites.

	Food		Coffee		Music		Movies/TV
	Books		Comedians		Clothes		People
	Cleanliness		Grammar		Brands		Soap
	Soda		Candy		_____		_____

Question Your Assumptions

What if there are more possibilities than you've experienced yet, and what if you actually really loved some of them? Look at the areas of pickiness that you checked off. Circle the ones in which you could perhaps try a new experience.

Will You Do It?

Where are you brave enough to actually try something new? If you're not picky about something, it doesn't take any courage to get out of your comfort zone. If you don't care about the feel of the toilet paper you use (although honestly, how can you *not* care about that??), then it's no big deal to use a different brand. But when you *are* picky, it takes bravery to consider something new.

Area of Pickiness	**New Things to Try**	**How Was It?**
Example:		
Food	*Dragon fruit, my friend's soup*	*Weird, not bad*
_____	_____	_____
_____	_____	_____
_____	_____	_____
_____	_____	_____
_____	_____	_____
_____	_____	_____
_____	_____	_____
_____	_____	_____

Now What?

Do you see the power of *considering*? Navigating change means you're moving from what you thought about the future to a new reality. No matter how big or how small the change, the biggest obstacle can be your willingness to consider that new reality.

Every time you ask yourself "what if . . ." you strengthen your resilience.

A NEW OPINION

PURPOSE: To open to the possibility that you could change your mind.

When science tells us something new, it's not that it lied to us before. It learned more now.

This truth is very hard for many people to swallow because we want predictability. Opening to the possibility that a belief we hold or a fact we learned (Hey, Pluto the planet meteor dwarf planet, how are you these days?) could change is tremendously uncomfortable. The uncomfortable reality is that many opinions, beliefs, and even learned facts do change over a lifetime.

The great news is that this ability—to change one's mind, to shift beliefs, to learn new, more accurate information—strengthens us.

What did you learn in school that has changed?

When you were in school, you may have learned about the nine planets of our solar system. You might have been taught that when typing you should put two spaces between sentences. You might have learned that European settlers were uniformly friendly and supportive to the native peoples of the lands they conquered and were welcomed by those people.

What did you learn then that you've learned more accurate or new information about since?

_____

_____

What beliefs have you shifted?

Are there things you see differently now or ideas you hold that are newer in your life? Many people explore belief systems in their teens and adulthood, finding a new idea they hadn't considered before to be a good fit or an older idea to no longer make sense to them.

Think back to your teen years. What beliefs did you hold then about:

Music:

_____

_____

Food:

_____

_____

Your Parents:

_____

_____

Education:

_____

_____

Religion:

_____

_____

Friends:

_____

_____

Politics:

_____

_____

Your Future:

_____

_____

Go back and circle any beliefs that have changed for you since then.

What unusual opinions do you hold?

I hate chicken. Not chickens. I tolerate those just fine. But if I'm coming to your house for dinner and you're serving chicken, I'm going to politely decline and eat a *lot* of side dish.

How about you? What fairly harmless thing do most people like just fine but you are not at all interested in?

_____

_____

What if you're wrong?

I don't mean what if you learned to tolerate classical music or scary movies or yoga or wine (you're maybe getting a glimpse of my personal beliefs) or whatever. I mean what if you hated, say, chicken, until you had some you really liked and discovered some types of cooked chicken are excellent and exactly what's been missing from your life?

Many people use the things they love and the things they hate to help define who they are in the world. And we get so attached to those aspects of our "personal brand" that we're afraid to question them and totally unwilling to change those opinions because we've aligned with them for so long they've become a part of our identity.

Which of your opinions are you willing to challenge?

_____

_____

How will you experiment to see if you still hold that opinion or if you've grown or changed in some way?

_____

_____

Now What?

Be really, truly proud of yourself. Opening to change like this is incredibly difficult. Most people see no reason to bother and stay in their comfort zone. You've learned how questioning your own picture of what is and what will be can make change so much easier to navigate.

In the next section we'll build the skill of managing all that discomfort so this just gets easier and easier to do.

YOU DID THAT!

WELL DONE! You strengthened your resilience by opening to change.

Here's another quick way to open to change. What is one thing you don't usually do at bedtime but you'd like to do? One thing that doesn't require you to spend any money or change anything fundamental in your life, just a new way of ending your day that might help you sleep better or feel good?

What is it? _____

Put an alarm in your phone now for about an hour before you expect to go to bed tonight reminding yourself to try it.

Now for the Best Part

You've done some hard work! Please follow this QR code by focusing your camera app on this code with your phone or tablet and clicking on the website that comes up.

Why?

Three reasons!

1. You can brag about a possibility you've considered that you never did before and see what changes other people have opened up to recently.
2. Grab your badge!
3. **There's a gift** for you to see what possibilities exist in your work, your life, your hobbies, even your fashion!

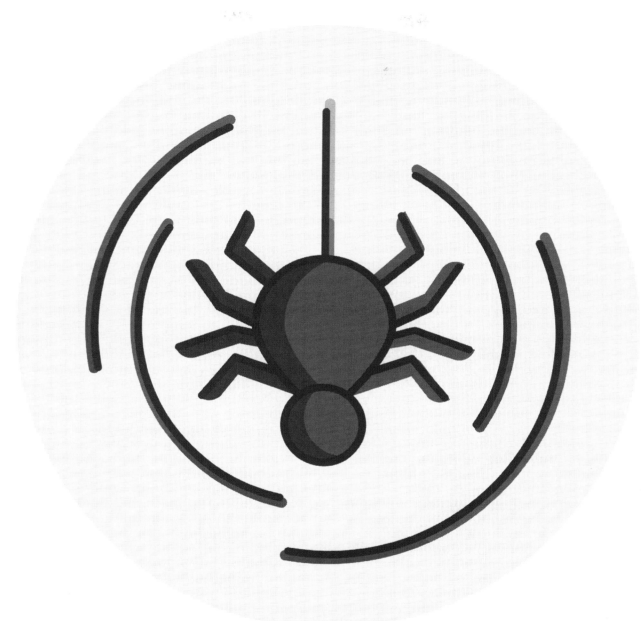

Manage Discomfort

MANAGE DISCOMFORT

IMAGINE IF YOU DIDN'T CARE ABOUT BEING UNCOMFORTABLE.
If you never noticed feeling a little hot or cold, somewhat hungry or kinda tired. What if public speaking was no big deal and rejection didn't make you sick to your stomach? What if disagreeing with your boss or arguing with a coworker or going for your employee review caused you no stress whatsoever?

What if you managed discomfort so well that you hardly even registered feeling that way?

Managing your own discomfort is key to feeling less stressed.

No matter what change you're navigating, it's the discomfort that is most likely to push you toward a negative outcome.

A Little Science (Just a little, I promise)

You've probably heard of adrenaline and cortisol. They're often called the "fight-or-flight-or-freeze hormones." These are the two chemicals our brains release when we feel threatened. Adrenaline makes the heart rate and blood pressure increase. Cortisol raises blood sugar and gets us to breathe faster and then helps the brain use the increased levels of glucose and oxygen. Cortisol also shuts down some of our body's systems so they don't interfere in handling whatever threat we're facing—like the gastrointestinal, immune, reproductive, and endocrine systems and even higher neural processing in the brain. When the perceived threat is gone, our body fairly quickly returns to normal.

This cascade of events is life-saving when we're truly in danger. So, when you start to cross at a busy intersection and your brain realizes (before you can even think the words) that there is a car coming at you, this cascade causes you to put everything you've got into jumping out of the way—and doesn't require a conscious decision to do that. Cortisol serves to shut down our ability to reason and plan so that we don't get in our own way. Fantastic.

The problem is that this cascade begins every time we feel threatened, not just every time we actually are threatened. And the chemicals don't dissolve if the feeling persists. If the feeling persists, then so does the elevated blood pressure, the increased blood sugar, the inhibited digestive system (which weirdly can cause constipation or diarrhea or both!), the suppressed immune system (hello, runny nose), the messed-up endocrine and reproductive hormones (worsening diabetes, thyroid issues, migraines, fatigue, weight gain).

Worst of all, if the feeling of being threatened persists, it continues to interfere with our ability to reason and plan.

Do you know what most often triggers that threatened state?

Stress.

When we feel stressed, our brains decide that we are threatened. The longer we feel the stress, or the more stress we perceive, the more our brains pump out the adrenaline and cortisol.

So how do we interrupt this cycle of stressor -> feeling threatened -> physical and emotional distress -> difficulty reasoning and planning?

We convince our brains to stop feeling threatened by learning to view stress differently.

This idea plays a central role in our conversation so far—seeing stress as a tool and not a toxin. The question is, then, how can we encounter stressors—events or people that make us feel threatened—and dial down that chemical cascade?

As we've talked about before, we often can't stop the stressors—the things that make us feel threatened—from coming at us.

Where we do have a lot of control is how we manage stressors when they do show up.

You're already an expert in this!

From the first time a baby cries, she is trying to figure out how to manage her discomfort and feel better. You already know a hundred ways to manage your own stress. Some of those ways are effective, some are healthy, some are neither of those things.

Managing your own discomfort is key to feeling less stressed.

We're going to focus in this section on how to expand your repertoire. The more options you have for managing your discomfort (in healthy and effective ways), the more stress can come at you without really bothering you. You'll notice it, and you'll know how to move it along.

This skill—managing discomfort—will allow you to navigate change the way you want to do it. Instead of choosing whatever path allows you to run from or fight against or freeze up in the face of change, you'll choose the path that sees beyond the stressor and gets you moving toward the life you want.

WALK, DON'T RUN

PURPOSE: Identify levels of discomfort and sort out what's actually dangerous.

Being uncomfortable is the worst! Except, it isn't.

In the last chapter we talked about how stress makes us feel threatened. That leads our brain to pump up the adrenaline and cortisol so that we have a big, strong reaction. That reaction makes us feel even more at risk, so we flee or fight or freeze up.

In order to interrupt this cycle, we have to figure out what deserves our cortisol and what doesn't and then learn how to ease ourselves down from feeling threatened.

It's crucial for us to sort out what is actually dangerous and what just *feels* dangerous because it's causing such a big reaction in our bodies.

Warning Signs

How do you know you're feeling stressed? What signs or symptoms does your body give you when your brain feels threatened? When you get an email that a client is unhappy or you learn that a complaint has been filed against you or you receive a voicemail from your doctor to call back about concerning test results . . .

What do you physically feel in these parts of your body?

Stomach: —————————————   Hands/Arms: —————————————

—————————————   —————————————

Chest: —————————————   Feet/Legs: —————————————

—————————————   —————————————

Head: —————————————

These are the short-term adrenaline and cortisol actions in your body.

When you're having a stressful day (or few days) with a lot on your mind, multiple worries, or stressors with no clear solution . . .

What do you notice about your:

Focus: —————————————   Memory: —————————————

—————————————   —————————————

Mood: —————————————   Thoughts: —————————————

—————————————   —————————————

Overall Health: —————————————

These are some of the long-term effects of adrenaline and cortisol.

Naming your own reactions will allow you to recognize much more quickly when you feel threatened so that you can ask the next, very important question:

Is My Brain Right about This?

When your brain feels threatened it has only one emergency signal. So you get the same "FREAK OUT RIGHT NOW DON'T DIE!" reaction no matter whether the stressor was a vague "we need to talk" message from your partner or a bang that wakes you in the middle of the night. Only one of these is life-threatening, but your brain gives you the same heart-pounding, can't-breathe feeling in each situation. So how do you figure out what is "just" discomfort—even if it's *really, really* uncomfortable—and what's actually dangerous?

First, let's define our terms:

UNCOMFORTABLE
(adjective, un-CUM-fer-tuh-bul) awkward, uneasy, causing pain or annoyance.

DANGEROUS
(adjective, DEYN-jer-uhs) potential for serious risk, causing injury or death, perilous, unsafe.

Now, let's play a game.

First make a list of at least twelve events or situations that stress you out. These can be from recent days, your past experiences, or concerns you have about the future.

Stressful Events or Situations:

_____   _____

_____   _____

_____   _____

_____   _____

Just Uncomfortable or Also Dangerous?

Uncomfortable   Actually Dangerous

_____   _____

_____   _____

_____   _____

_____   _____

_____   _____

How Uncomfortable Is It?

Once you've identified something as dangerous, use your cortisol and adrenaline for good! Save your life! Act!

Once you've identified something as uncomfortable (maybe even really, really uncomfortable) but not actually dangerous, get yourself some perspective.

Rate it on a scale from 1 to 10.

I'm a doctor, and we're always asking people to rate their pain on a scale from one to ten. The reason for that is because pain has levels; some pain needs immediate attention and some we can distract ourselves from or manage in different ways. Also, that scale helps us measure improvement or worsening.

Go back to your "uncomfortable" list from above and copy those down here, and add some if you'd like. Then rate the discomfort you feel from that event or situation by circling a number from one ("Eh, I don't love it but no big deal") to ten ("I hate this and can't think about anything else even for a second!").

Uncomfortable Event or Situation

_____ 1 2 3 4 5 6 7 8 9 10

_____ 1 2 3 4 5 6 7 8 9 10

_____ 1 2 3 4 5 6 7 8 9 10

_____ 1 2 3 4 5 6 7 8 9 10

_____ 1 2 3 4 5 6 7 8 9 10

_____ 1 2 3 4 5 6 7 8 9 10

_____ 1 2 3 4 5 6 7 8 9 10

_____ 1 2 3 4 5 6 7 8 9 10

By rating discomfort, we get our brains out of the all-or-nothing paradigm that causes us to release all those stress chemicals. We engage our reasoning and slow down from a run to a walk in our reactions.

Good, Necessary, or Just Bad?

Not all uncomfortable situations are valuable. Some are useful, with lots to teach us and much to gain. Some are unavoidable. And some are just annoying or damaging with no benefit at the end. Before we discover how to manage the discomfort we feel, it's really helpful to consider which situations to walk away from instead.

Grab your pen

Go back to that list of uncomfortable and mark it up. Next to each uncomfortable event or situation, put U, N, U/N or X next to it, following this key:

U—Useful (There is growth or learning here or potential for a good outcome.)

N—Necessary (You have no choice but to deal with this situation.)

U/N—Useful and Necessary

X—This is just annoying and you could choose to walk away from it.

Now What?

As you begin to think about your own reactions to stress, this exercise can help you utilize your big reactions only when they're helpful. That way, you can decrease the number of times and ways you feel that level of threat and learn how to discriminate between dangerous and uncomfortable.

The rest of this section is devoted to helping you manage that discomfort, so you can move your number down the scale from "I hate this and I can't think about anything else!" to "Eh, I don't love it, but it's not a big deal."

MINING YOUR OWN EXPERIENCE

PURPOSE: Identify and grow your strategies for managing discomfort.

How old are you? That is how many years of experience you have managing your own discomfort. Since you were a baby and felt cold or hungry or wet or tired and opened your mouth to yell about it, you've been looking for ways to feel better when you don't like how you feel.

You've learned tons about what makes you feel better in the years since then.

What Do You Do?

First, it's time to discover your current practices. Some of these are great, and some are unhealthy. Some you brag about, and some you hope nobody notices or ever finds out about. For this first list, take away *all* your judgment and just write down everything you can think of that you do when you don't like how you feel. Think about what you eat or drink, what you watch, what games or hobbies or activities you turn to in those moments. Remember that this list is just for you. Make as long a list as you can!

What do you do when you don't like how you feel?

_____

_____

_____

_____

_____

_____

Can't think of anything else? Sure you can! Think about how you speak to other people and how you talk to yourself. Do you encourage yourself or list your faults? Do you ask for hugs or support or snap at your colleagues and yell at your loved ones? Is it all that and more? Go back up and add to the list.

Feeling really brave? Ask the people you live with or those who know you best. "What behaviors or activities do I do when I'm unhappy or uncomfortable or worried?" Add those! I hope you need another piece of paper because the longer the list, the more effective this activity will be.

Do No Harm

Physicians take an oath to "First, do no harm." I really want you to take that oath as well. So go back through that list and scratch out all the actions or behaviors that hurt you or someone else. Now it's time to use your judgment. Again, no one else will see this list. This is for *you*.

Did you identify something that worries you?

That can be a frightening or frustrating feeling. I'm sorry you're experiencing that. But it's a huge show of strength and resilience to be able to notice if you have a risky behavior and get some help to manage it. So please, if you notice anything that concerns you, contact your doctor or another trusted professional and let them know what is going on with you.

What do you do when you don't like how you feel that doesn't hurt you or anyone else?

_____

_____

_____

_____

_____

These are your **positive and neutral coping mechanisms.** These are all things you currently know how to do to manage your discomfort. All of these will take your Uncomfortable Scale Number (from the last exercise) down a notch or two or eight.

Add to the List!

If you already believed that these coping mechanisms were totally sufficient, you probably wouldn't have chosen this section to work on today. You want more, and more effective, ways to manage your discomfort. That's great news because the longer _this_ list is, the less discomfort you will feel when you navigate change.

Where can you find new ideas?

What have you considered trying? Is there something you've heard or imagined helps reduce stress but you haven't gotten around to trying it? Like knitting or boxing or deep breathing or painting or yelling on a mountaintop or stacking rocks?

_____

_____

_____

What do you see in people you know? Think about the people in your life whom you relate to or respect. What do you see them do that seems to help them feel better?

_____

_____

_____

What strategies can you steal from famous people? What (free or cheap) ideas can you grab from the celebrities you watch, the podcasters you listen to, the authors you read? Most everyone who's been interviewed has talked about ways they do what they do. Go look for some tools they use to decrease stress that sound like something that could work for you.

_____

_____

_____

Now What?

Use this list. When you feel uncomfortable or worried or scared or sad or angry, and you know that the situation is necessary or useful, come to this list and use your tools to manage your discomfort. This will decrease your adrenaline and cortisol so that you will be better able to reason and plan your way forward.

TAKE
A LESSON

PURPOSE: Practice managing your discomfort and remembering why it's worth it.

Being uncomfortable is hard, but it's often useful or necessary: *necessary* if the event or the situation is unavoidable, *useful* if we can grow or learn something we need. If it's neither of those things, then we don't have to suffer. We can walk away.

In order to build strength for the times when being uncomfortable is necessary or useful, practice really helps.

Don't worry. Practice can be *fun*!

What Would Be Useful?

If you're going to put yourself in an uncomfortable position on purpose (and you are, just trust me), then that discomfort should benefit you. In addition to strengthening you, there should be some other reward.

Brainstorm a list of things you've always wanted to try or to learn or to get better at doing. I'll start: doing my taxes (must save money), glass blowing (it looks so cool), photography, growing things, baking, and hang gliding. Your turn:

_____

_____

_____

What Might Be Fun?

OK, taxes are out. Narrow that list to a few things that you think you'd actually enjoy once you learned how to do it.

_____

_____

_____

Go. Do. It.

I'm serious. Find a class and take one lesson. Most schools and centers that teach stuff will let you take one class for free (even if they don't advertise that, ask!). Try hard to find a class that has other people in it.

What's Hard about Learning This New Thing?

Let's face it. I said, "Go. Do. It." and some part of your brain said, "No!" You thought about what you'd lose. Money? Time? Comfort? You didn't trust that you could or should do it or that it would be worth the struggle. You thought about just how uncomfortable it might be to tell other people you were doing it, to set aside the time to do it, or to actually take a lesson in something you've never learned before. Remember the Resilience Cycle?

All change causes stress. Loss, distrust, and discomfort are the natural reactions to change.

What Might Be Good about Learning This New Thing?

I'm actually asking. Whatever skill or experience you're considering, what are the benefits? Fun is one, right? You already checked for that. What else? Imagine learning to do this new skill. What would be good about that?

FUN...

_____

_____

Remembering why we're doing something makes it much easier to push through the hard parts.

We tolerate discomfort better when the purpose is clear.

So Go. Do. It!

Pick one of the fun, useful skills and sign up right now to take one lesson in it.

When is it scheduled?

_____

What are you nervous about?

_____

What can you do when those things you're nervous about happen?

Go to Exercise 14 and scan through your positive and neutral coping mechanisms. Which ones would help you leading up to or during the class to manage your discomfort (other than leaving the class)?

_____

_____

_____

Now What?

Want some more ways to practice managing your discomfort when it's your choice and fun? All of these are guaranteed to be uncomfortable and worthwhile for most people. Try any of these:

- **Practice a language.** Do you know a little of any other language? Spend a little time with someone who is fluent in that language and patient. Ask them to let you practice with them.
- **New foods.** Order or cook an entire meal of foods you've never tried before. Eat at least a little of each.
- **Seek out the opposition.** Whatever source you use for news, find an outlet (TV, online, whatever) that you believe to be biased in a way you don't like. Listen to an entire news program and see if you can identify why some people agree.
- **Root for a sports team from a place you don't like in a sport you love.** They don't have to be playing against your team, just go root for the "enemy" for one game and see how you feel
- **Volunteer to speak if you usually don't.** The next time you're at a meeting for work, in your town, or at your kid's school and they ask for comments, step up and add your opinion.
- **Be quiet if you're usually not.** The next time you're at a meeting for work, in your town, or at your kid's school and they ask for comments, sit and listen to others instead of speaking out.
- **Don't interrupt a sad story.** Listen to a coworker or a friend or your child tell you about something hard that happened to them. Don't interrupt even once. At the end, offer empathy without any suggestions or solutions.

LOOK HOW FAR YOU'VE COME!

PURPOSE: Recognize the strength you've developed and renew your determination to get more resilience faster.

Let's Jump in the Wayback Machine.

What's today's date?⋆

_____

*not a trick question, just write the date

What was the day on this date five years ago? (just do the math)

_____

What was happening in your life then?

Picture things this month but five years ago. How old were you? Where did you work? Where were you living? How old were your siblings or your kids? Were you dating or married at the time? Were you planning a vacation? What big projects were you working on? Got an image in your mind of where you were physically, emotionally, financially, etc.? Good.

Now think about the biggest stressor you faced that month. Imagine we were good friends and I ran into you then.

Me: Hey, my friend. How are you?

Five-years-ago You: _____

Me: I'm so glad to see you! You seem a little stressed. What's hard right now?

Five-years-ago You (being really honest):

_____

_____

_____

Me: I'm so sorry you're going through that. Help me understand a little more. On a scale of one to ten,* how bad is it?

1 2 3 4 5 6 7 8 9 10

(1 is a little bit stressful, 10 is the absolute worst)

*Yes, I do sometimes ask my friends this question. You can feel sorry for them!

What Doesn't Kill You . . . Usually Makes You Miserable

Even though we're not that kind of friends (yet), I really am sorry you went through that. It was hard, and you struggled with it. I'm glad you survived it, but survival alone doesn't make something worthwhile. I hope it turned out to be useful, but even if it was just necessary, I'm glad you can look back on it five years later because it may have been a little bit useful in a way you haven't considered.

Where Are You Now?

Imagine that same stressor you faced five years ago showing up in your life now. How bad would it be? Consider all you currently know, having the connections and boundaries and experiences you've acquired in the past five years.

If that stressor came up again now, how bad would it feel?

1 2 3 4 5 6 7 8 9 10

(1 is a little bit stressful, 10 is the absolute worst)

Accidental Strength

You are stronger today than you were five years ago. You have more skills to manage your discomfort. You do learn from every difficult experience, even when you're not paying attention.

On the other hand, we all know people who've gone through tons of hard things and it never seems to get any easier for them. That's the problem with accidental growth—it doesn't always happen and even when it occurs, it doesn't benefit you nearly as much as it could with some intentionality.

To go back to the exercise analogy I'm so fond of, it's like wandering around a parking lot because you lost your car. It *is* getting some steps in, but it's not really a fitness plan. This "accidental" growth is growth. It's worth noticing and being proud of when you think of all you've managed so far in your life. You just shouldn't have to rely on adversity to build your resilience.

Building resilience intentionally works faster and hurts less than just surviving.

Be proud of all you've learned. Be wildly impressed with yourself that you've decided to stop leaving your own growth and resilience to chance!

Now What?

If you're a "go through the book in order" kind of person, congratulations! You're halfway through! The next group of skills will have purpose, fun, and autonomy baked in. All of those make it easier for people to succeed. Thank you, sincerely, for the work you've done so far. You're already stronger than you were at the beginning of this book. That intentional growth will get you more resilience and will get it faster than ever before.

YOU DID THAT!

BRAVO! You strengthened your resilience by figuring out how to better manage discomfort.

Question for you. Was it uncomfortable to tackle this chapter?

____ Yes ____ No

When I speak to audiences, this is the skill that causes the most people to say "Help! I need that!"

Even if it was uncomfortable, you did it anyway. **What did you do to manage those feelings?**

_____

_____

_____

Be proud of yourself—managing discomfort is one of the hardest things for humans to do.

Now for the Best Part

You deserve a reward for all that! Please follow this QR code by focusing your camera app on this code with your phone or tablet and clicking on the website that comes up.

Why?

Three reasons!

1. You have some discomfort managing strategies that could help someone else. You could really help a person you don't even know by sharing a couple of your tips.
2. Get your badge!
3. There's a gift for you to grow your own list of positive and neutral coping mechanisms from business and world leaders!

Set Goals

SET
GOALS

WANT TO SEE A TEENAGER'S EYES GLAZE OVER? Ask this question:

"What do you want to be when you grow up?"

Forget the part about how it's patronizing—because most teens feel pretty grown up already and don't love anyone pointing out that they might not be—and focus on the scope of that question. It's *huge.* How is a seventeen-year-old supposed to know what they are aiming for—even "just" professionally—for the *rest of their life*?

It's the wrong question (more on that in Exercise 20) but it's a really important and valuable question too.

Decades of research have shown that asking a student about their goals does, in fact, help them perform better academically (with some follow-up). Further, asking kids about the careers they're thinking of also increases their likelihood of having a career and not just a series of low-paying jobs.

It's Not Just Kids

Through validated scientific investigation, adults have been proven to achieve success (as they themselves define it) far more readily when they have stated goals. Success rates go up if you write down those goals. Even higher if you break up those big goals into action steps.

It's Not Just about Success

Goals increase your chance of achievement sometimes. They increase your personal growth and resilience all the time.

> "What you **get** by achieving your goals is not as important as what you **become** by achieving your goals."
>
> — Henry David Thoreau (1817–1862)

At the risk of inserting myself into these wise words, my own research would lead me to add an idea:

What you get by *achieving* your goals is not as important as what you become by *pursuing* them.

Goals drive your direction, for sure. They tell you where to aim.

Goals fuel your motivation because goals remind you of your purpose.

And . . .

Goals Build Your Resilience

Remember those things our brains focus on when we encounter change?

Navigating loss, distrust, and discomfort is *hard.* Having a purpose—a goal—helps us manage that discomfort by reminding us why it is worth the struggle. Goals help us answer the questions that come up in the midst of stress:

- Why is this happening?
- Why am I doing this?
- Why not give up?

Goals help you navigate change and come through it with integrity and purpose because goals clarify your purpose!

Dive into these exercises to practice setting goals that push you toward happiness and fulfillment. Because that's where you'll find your purpose.

WHAT DO YOU WANT OUT OF LIFE?

PURPOSE: To identify your big-picture reasons for living.

Why build resilience? So that you can navigate all the change and stress that comes at you in life and come through it the kind of person you want to be. So we have to ask ourselves: What kind of person *do* you want to be?

You can't succeed at being resilient—or anything—if you don't know what success means to you. Consider a game a friend is teaching you. They explain the rules and tell you to try to win. Well, you have to know what "winning" looks like, right?

What Does Winning Mean to You?

Don't be distracted or frustrated by the scope of this question because you already know these answers.

What are your top five priorities?

Don't think too hard this first time through the question. Consider your own well-being, the people who matter to you, and the purpose you want to serve in life, and don't try to put them in order of importance.

- _____

- _____

- _____

- _____

- _____

Check Your Work

Now think for a minute about the end of your life. What do you want to look back on and know you created or supported or accomplished? What relationships do you want to sustain? How long do you want to live (meaning, are you prioritizing your own health)? Are you factoring in your own dreams? Are you considering the people with whom you share love? When you rock on the porch at age ninety and think about your life, what will matter? We've all seen movies and read books about people who look back on their lives, sorry for their choices. Goals help you look back with satisfaction.

You can regret-proof the end of your life by considering your priorities now.

With that in mind, copy over or rewrite your priorities:

- _____

- _____

- _____

- _____

- _____

From Priorities to Goals

Priorities are not actions or even targets. Priorities reflect your values and your dreams, but they don't offer much of a roadmap for how to get there. Priorities ask, "What matters to you?" Goals state what you want. Let me show you an example of what I mean.

One of my top five priorities is for sure my four sons. Not just "family," but my boys, in particular, get their own line in my list. They're my priority, so now I have to ask: What do I want from or for or with them? What's the goal? For me, the goal is

"Enjoy time with my sons." See the difference between priority and goal?

Another of my top five priorities is increasing resilience. Not just for me, but for everyone. That's my priority, so what do I want from that or for that or with that? My goal is "Create a more resilient society."

We'll get to more specifics in a minute, but first, please do this work. Copy over your priorities and figure out what your goal is for each:

Your Priorities

What Do You Want from or with That Priority?

_____   _____

_____   _____

_____   _____

_____   _____

Now take a deep breath. You just did something really hard! You identified—for now—your priorities and goals in life. If you've got the nagging feeling that you missed something or might change your mind, that's OK! Priorities *do* change and goals *do* shift. What's important is that you take the time to figure out what matters to you, so you can navigate change and keep moving toward the life you really want!

How Do You Get What You Want?

These goals are *huge*. The only way to get them is by breaking them down into the smaller pieces that will get you there.

My goal is to "Enjoy time with my sons." To do that I need to do several things. I need to make sure my schedule allows for the time I want. I need to communicate with each of my boys to find things they actually want to do together. I need to raise them to be people I can enjoy as adults. I need to be comfortable with them making their own decisions in life so that I don't waste our time together trying to tell them what to do. I need to earn enough money to be able to go see them wherever life takes them.

Every goal has tasks or smaller goals underneath it that are necessary to get there. We'll focus on how to break down big goals into small goals and actually accomplish them in the rest of this section.

Now What?

You now have a way to double-check your own decision-making. When you are offered an opportunity or consider making a move, you can ask yourself if that opportunity or move is aligned with your priorities, if it moves you toward or away from your goals.

WEEKEND GOALS

Purpose: Define a short-term goal and translate it to small, actionable steps.

What Do You Want?

This coming weekend, what do you want? Forget for a minute about what you have scheduled or planned, and just picture Sunday evening. What do you want to feel by the time you get in bed Sunday night? Not a rhetorical question.

What words do you want to use Sunday night to describe how you feel?

_____

_____

_____

Goal Translation

A key to using goal-setting skills to strengthen resilience is translating the feeling you want into the goal that can get you there. For example, you might have said that you want to lie down Sunday night and feel relaxed. Or satisfied. Or happy. Or bored! Whatever the feeling you're aiming toward, now you have to figure out what you have to *do* to get that feeling.

What would you have to do this weekend to get that feeling by Sunday night?

_____

_____

_____

Is that really possible in a weekend? And does it align with your life priorities? Even if you're not sure *how exactly* you'd get it done, decide if your answer is actually possible in one weekend. Consider other obligations you have, like sleep or feeding the younger (or older) humans who live in your home or having clean clothes for next week, and look at it again. With all that in mind (your answer doesn't have to change):

What would you have to do this weekend to get that feeling by Sunday night?

_____

_____

_____

☞☞☞ is your Big Goal. Circle or highlight it please. We're coming back to it.

Big goals can feel terrible until you look at them more closely.

Figuring Out the Ingredients

If you woke up Saturday morning and just thought, "OK, time to do my Big Goal," you'd be unlikely to succeed. For the same reason that 75 percent of New Year's resolutions get ditched before MLK Day, Big Goals fail us. You need a map to get you to that Big Goal. And we need an example to understand this. Rewind with me to the beginning of this exercise, and I'll show you what I mean.

What words do you want to use Sunday night to describe how you feel?

Calm, more organized, less like home is out of control.

What would you have to do this weekend to get that feeling by Sunday night?
Get rid of all the clothes that everyone has grown out of, clean out the closet in the storage area, and fold or hang everything.

Is that really possible in a weekend?

What would you have to do this weekend to get that feeling by Sunday night?
Get rid of all the clothes that everyone has grown out of.

OK, now I've caught up to you. Now let's work on this side by side.

What are the steps that are necessary to reach your Big Goal?

Me:

1. Go through child #1 room w/him

2. Go through child #2 room

3. Go through other kids' rooms

4. Go through my room

5. Put giveaway stuff in bags

6. Put big kids' stuff in storage

7. Drop off at Goodwill

You:

1. _____

2. _____

3. _____

4. _____

5. _____

6. _____

7. _____

Schedule It In

Each of these steps is a little easier to accomplish than the full Big Goal, but time and goals can still get away from us. Now that we've decided what, we need to decide when. Be honest with yourself about how long this might take you and the other people involved, and remember that you need to get to Sunday night with enough energy to start the week!

When will you do it?

Me:

1. Child #1 room Sat 8a-11a

2. Child #2 room Sat 12n-2p

3. Child #3 & #4 room Sat 3p-6p

4. My room Sun 10a-noon

5. Stuff in bags Sun 1p-2p

6. Stuff to storage Sun 2p-3p

7. Drop @ Goodwill Sun before 5p

You:

1. _____

2. _____

3. _____

4. _____

5. _____

6. _____

7. _____

Scratch It Off!

Don't underestimate the power of working through your list. Keep this exercise handy and, as you accomplish a step, cross it off. Give yourself breaks. Try to beat your own clock. If, like me, you need other people to help, challenge them to finish doing a good job early so that you can relax together for the rest of that time slot. And come back to this page Sunday night.

How do you actually feel?

_____

_____

Now What?

Any goal, no matter how overwhelming or how straightforward, can be broken into steps. The smaller the steps, the more likely you are to accomplish them. That feeling of accomplishment is a tool that can easily motivate you toward the next step. Don't forget this strategy when you're feeling overwhelmed.

#RELATIONSHIP GOALS

PURPOSE: To determine what goals are within your control and how to shift your focus there.

You Have Needs

In Exercise 17, I asked you about your priorities. Did you put any other people or relationships on that list? If so, this exercise is for you.

Who did you put on your priority list?

_____

What goal do you want with that person or group or relationship? Write down what you wrote in Exercise 17:

_____

That's a Big Goal. When we have big goals that involve other people, we face some obstacles. For example, if you said that your spouse or partner is a priority, then maybe your Big Goal is to live a long and happy life with that person. Great goal, right? Some of that you can directly affect, and some is out of your control.

A key to resilience is determining what is within your control, focusing there, and simply observing what is not.

Are You Where You Want to Be?

Think of someone in your life who is important to you: a good friend, a parent, a sibling, a partner, a child, anyone who is a priority for you. Pick someone with whom things are a little rocky right now or the relationship isn't what you think it could be.

Which relationship would you like to improve?

Relationships are dynamic—they are always changing. Consider how things are between you and this person right now. Rate that relationship on these three metrics:

This month, how connected do you feel to this person?

1   2   3   4   5   6   7   8   9   10

(1 is hardly connected at all, 10 is totally in sync)

This month, how comfortable do you feel when you're with or talking to this person?

1   2   3   4   5   6   7   8   9   10

(1 is very uncomfortable, 10 is the most comfortable you can feel)

This month, how happy do you feel when you're with or talking to this person?

1   2   3   4   5   6   7   8   9   10

(1 is very unhappy, 10 is extremely happy)

Every relationship goes through easy times and hard times. Sometimes the relationship is really excellent but not so happy or comfortable while someone in it deals with outside stressors. Sometimes you're blissfully happy in a relationship but you're in a time of less connection while one person is traveling, or you're very connected and happy but not so comfortable with the way a person is changing.

It's not necessary to be at (or get to) a ten on each of these scales. It's necessary to figure out if your scales are where *you* need them to be, and if not, what you can do to improve the situation.

Defining What You Can Control

I asked you to pick someone with whom things aren't at their best right now.

What could be better?

_____

_____

_____

OK, now for the really hard part. If that person didn't change a *thing* about their behavior or attitude, what could you do to improve the situation? Don't think about them meeting you halfway, and don't think about them having a sudden understanding of how awesome you are, or how much they need you.

What can *you* do to improve the situation between you?

_____

_____

_____

Which of those things are you willing to do? Pick one that is entirely within your control and doesn't require them to all of a sudden be happier or more open or more accommodating. Circle the one you're willing to do.

_____

_____

_____

Observing, Not "Letting Go"

You can't make someone else change their mood, their attitude, or their behavior. You can't, in short, make them *do* anything at all. You can only change your own mood, attitude, and behaviors, and even that takes a lot of work.

There's a lot of advice out there to "let go" of what you can't control. That's incredibly difficult to do because it implies that you stop caring about what other people say or do or how they act. In a priority relationship, it's not useful—or often possible—to stop caring. The good news? You don't have to "let go" in order to stop trying to control things that are beyond your control.

Shift to observing. Just notice that person's moods, attitudes, and behaviors and how they affect you. Work on managing your discomfort when you don't like how you feel. Set good boundaries, like how much time you spend or what you choose to do with that person. Build connections by respectfully communicating what your needs are and what you can offer. Keep reminding yourself what you *can* control and focus there.

Reaching your goals requires you to focus on your own actions, not wait for others to become what you wish they would.

Now What?

As you consider your goals in any situation, bring this lesson into your mind. Are you waiting for someone else to take an action? Have you been waiting long enough and want to find some options (more on this in the Take Action section) that don't depend on that someone? Is there an action you can take that will move things forward?

WHAT PROBLEM DO YOU WANT TO SOLVE?

PURPOSE: To take one life goal and find the building blocks you need to get it.

Remember that eye-glazing question that people often ask teens, "What do you want to be when you grow up?" I mentioned that this is the wrong question to ask, and the reason for that is . . . scope.

Contemplating what you want to "be" at any age is either such a wide and deep question that it's impossible to answer or it's such a wide and deep answer that it's nearly impossible to attain.

When trying to set and reach a goal, a much easier question to answer is:

"What problem do you want to solve first?" I'll show you what I mean.

Pick a Priority and Its Goal

Go on back to Exercise 17 (**What Do You Want Out of Life?**) and pick one of those priorities to work on in this exercise.

What's your priority?

_____

What do you want from or with that priority?

_____

Identify the Building Blocks

Look at the goal you just wrote down. What do you need to do differently or keep working on in order to reach that goal? Let's do this side by side. I'm going to focus on the priority, my health. What I want from or with that is to be able to travel with and engage in fun outdoor activities with my friends and family as far into old age as possible.

What do you need to do differently or keep working on to get there?

Me:

You:

1. Keep walking daily

1. _____

2. Improve strength and balance

2. _____

3. Do whatever possible to protect my health

3. _____

4. Find friends who like being active

4. _____

Find the Problems

Doing something differently is a pretty big ask. Continuing a behavior you already have is not usually difficult, but stopping that behavior and switching to a new one can be challenging. Look at your list of things to work on and poke around for the problems you need to solve to create those building blocks you just identified. Let's do it together. Refer to your list above for your numbers one to four (or higher if you added more).

What problems do you need to solve to do each of these things?

Me: You:

1. Walking   1. _____
   -boring, easy to quit

2. Strength and balance   2. _____
   -don't know how to improve

3. Protect health   3. _____
   -don't know what to do

4. Active friends   4. _____
   -many friends don't like this

Solving the Problems

It may seem discouraging to focus on the obstacles, but now we're getting from something we *want* to something we can actually *do*.

What are possible solutions to each of these problems?

Me: You:

1. Walking is boring   1. _____
   -partner, trainer, app,
   listen to something

2. Improve strength and balance   2. _____
   -videos, trainer, PT, gym
   -ask friends in better shape

3. Protect health how?   3. _____
   -get osteoporosis test
   -get colonoscopy, mammogram
   -immunizations? Vitamins?
   -ask my doctor

4. Few active friends   4. _____
   -ask more friends about this
   -find new friends :)

Which Problem Do You Want to Solve First?

Achieving a huge goal is overwhelming, just as overwhelming as deciding at age sixteen what you want to "be" for your whole life. Picking a problem you want to solve—just one—is totally manageable. Even better? It's much more successful!

Think it through and call on your own expertise in yourself. Would you be more successful tackling first the one that seems hardest to you? Would it help you to knock out a much easier problem to get you started? Will you be happier in the process if you start with one that involves someone else, so they can cheer you on? Let's both commit. Go up, look at the list of problems you need to solve to reach this goal, and pick one.

What problem do you want to solve first?

Me: You:

Improve strength and balance   _____

What specifically will you do to solve that?

Me: You:

Work out to YouTube strength   _____
and balance videos 3x/week

Now What?

This process is really sweat-rinse-repeat. Every time you set a goal, take the time to define the building blocks, identify the obstacles, and commit to tackling one problem at a time. You'll be amazed at the resilience you will build!

Also—let's stop asking kids what they want to be when they grow up and start asking what problem in the world they'd like to solve first!

YOU DID THAT!

BRAVA! You strengthened your resilience by setting some goals.

I've got one more for you. What skill is your next goal? Having worked on some of this book, what skill would be most useful to you next?

_____

If you need to, go back to the table of contents you created in the Introduction and change it to suit your needs now.

Now for the Best Part

You've thought about some important stuff! Please follow this QR code by focusing your camera app on this code with your phone or tablet and clicking on the website that comes up.

Why?

Three reasons!

1. Tell someone a goal of yours and see what other people are aiming for next.
2. Grab your badge!
3. **There's a gift** for you: apps that can help you track your progress toward a goal. Pick the one that is right for you!

Find Options

FIND
OPTIONS

AS A DOCTOR, I'M IN THE OPTIONS BUSINESS.

You come to see me for a stomachache, I consider the options.

What could be causing it? Constipation, acid reflux, hernia, gallbladder disease, gastroparesis, tumor, mesenteric adenitis, malabsorption, ulcer, or dozens of other gastrointestinal issues. Not only that, I need to consider possible cardiac, musculoskeletal, urinary, or reproductive concerns, and even psychiatric problems.

So I ask lots of questions and poke and prod you a bit.

It's not usually as hard as it sounds, but as soon as I start to ignore options, I can miss things. We have this saying in medicine: "Common things are common." That's true, and the usual options are most often correct. But ignoring the less common options means I can miss opportunities to help you feel better sooner or catch something dangerous before it gets worse. I don't chase down every option I consider; my twenty years of experience in medicine have helped me know what to address first and what to keep in the back of my mind for later if you're not getting better.

We call this long list of possibilities a "differential diagnosis," and we reprimand any medical student or resident who can't make this list long and filled with rare options. Why?

You can't find what you don't look for, and you can't look for what you haven't considered.

This is true way beyond the exam room.

Consider the people whom you want to do business with. You work at a marketing and design company. You see that a LinkedIn connection of yours is looking to redesign their website. Great news, this person *loves* you—you've met a few times and really hit it off, and they've said twice that they'd love to work with you someday and hope your paths cross to do that. You reach out by phone, and this person tells you they've already signed a contract with a competitor. Why? "I thought you just did logos! We have a logo we like, so we don't need that. Oh, I'm so disappointed. I'd have loved to have worked with you!"

Ugh!

This person didn't know that you do much more than "just" logos, and they didn't look in order to find out. Now you're both frustrated, opportunity missed. They didn't find your services because they didn't look for them, and they didn't look because they hadn't even considered what they didn't know.

We need to consider that we don't know all our options—even when we think we do.

There is another obstacle to seeking out options. This problem is identified by social scientists as the "Paradox of Choice." There are many studies demonstrating that when we have a lot of options, we often walk away rather than make a decision. We'll tackle this in Section 7: Take Action. The reality, though, is that—while option overload is absolutely real—we are less resilient when we perceive that we have fewer choices.

Consider how stuck you feel when you're in a situation and can't see a way out. You can have the same feeling when you're trying to make a change but you don't know all the options for how to go about it.

Every time we experience a change, our brain focuses on loss, distrust, and discomfort, remember?

But as soon as we remember that we have choices, we start to act in a resilient way. We have to remember that we have multiple choices and start to figure out what those options are before we can pick the one(s) we want to try.

Options make us more resilient, because they help us navigate change and come through it with integrity and purpose. You've decided on a goal, and you've hit an obstacle or twelve on the way there. Now it's time to figure out the answer to a question one of my residency professors would ask every time we presented a case:

"OK, people. What are our options?"

WHAT ELSE?

PURPOSE: Stretch yourself to practice finding more possibilities.

What's your favorite number?

Don't think hard, just write down your lucky number: _____

You're playing a game, and someone already took that number. What other numbers do you really like? Pick three more. Yes, seriously, three more.

_____   _____   _____

What's your favorite color?

You're at a paint-your-own pottery party for a friend. It's time to choose the glaze or color you'll paint this bowl or mug . . . what do you pick?

_____

Oh! So sorry, we're out of that color! What are three other colors you like enough to look at on your counter every day?

_____   _____   _____

Favorite ice cream flavor?

If you don't like ice cream, write down your favorite dessert. And if you don't like dessert,

I'm offering you lots of empathy and suggesting you write down your favorite snack.

_____

Besides that flavor, what other flavors of ice cream would you be happy to eat? Or dessert or snack . . .

_____   _____   _____

What is something you won't compromise on?

For me, it's tea. I'd rather not drink tea at all if I can't have the kind I like prepared exactly the way I like. How about you?

_____

For what else do you like what you like and are not interested in "options"?

_____   _____   _____

Why Is This Hard?

When you "can't" have your first choice, how hard is it for you to think of more possibilities?

1   2   3   4   5   6   7   8   9   10

(1 is super easy, 10 is you totally gave up before you got to three more options)

People often struggle to think of more options, not because they aren't creative or open-minded or smart enough. We struggle because of *loss*.

Finding other options means you risk "losing" the first choice. Even if we've been told that our first choice isn't available, our brain resists the change and focuses on that loss. Considering more options feels like giving in or admitting defeat.

Finding options makes us more resilient because it helps us navigate change more easily. Ironically, though, finding options also *requires* resilience because it forces a change that we have to navigate from what we thought we'd pick or what we thought was happening to a world with other possible outcomes.

Now What?

If you haven't taken a stroll through Section 3: Open to Change, this might be a good time to go have a look. Finding options gets lots easier when we're open to new ideas.

As you go through your day today, or your week, find a few places to identify some options. Lunch order? The way you greet someone? The step you take first for a project? Your morning routine? Your plans for the evening? Of course you can go with the original plan. Just take a minute to build your option-identifying resilience first.

FIND MORE FUNNY

PURPOSE: To practice finding options you hadn't considered.

The world's oldest joke, dated to approximately thirty-nine thousand years ago, was a fart joke. Humor experts (university professors, seriously!) have collected jokes from every culture and time period, and here's what they've discovered:

Most jokes center around whatever a society considers really uncomfortable.

Anything considered rude, embarrassing, painful, private, personal, or downright disgusting hit the top of the joke list—and if you can combine some of those, even better.

Humans use humor to build connections, manage our discomfort, and find options.

A Little Laugh Science

Laughing releases two chemicals that flood our brains with good feelings. Endorphins are the natural chemical that binds to opioid receptors and gives a narcotic-like rush—without the terrible effects of using an actual narcotic. Laughter also triggers the release of serotonin, the brain's natural antidepressant.

Laughter with another person increases oxytocin—the bonding chemical that makes us feel more connected to others—and encourages us to seek out our people. This explains why so many of us look around for someone to tell when we see something funny!

These chemical reactions also explain why we make a joke or search for one when we're feeling uncomfortable. These hormones reduce the cortisol and adrenaline we *don't* like and give us a feeling we do like. So (I hope) it makes sense that we can use humor to strengthen us when we're struggling.

How Does Laughter Grow Our Resilience?

Even better than strengthening our resilience in a moment of extreme discomfort, laughter builds our resilience in every situation because of the unique puzzle in every funny moment.

Our brains have to figure out what's funny.

Understanding why we, or others, are laughing is a big communication puzzle. Is it laughter due to confusion? Silliness? Wonder? Is it laughing *at* someone or something, or is it encouragement? Is it laughter from a touch that tickles or a situation that shocks? These calculations begin subconsciously as soon as we notice that something is funny, to ourselves or anyone, and they happen very quickly.

When we notice humor, we have to process as many possibilities as we can about what is causing it. We keep searching for options. That practice, even when we're just watching a TV show or reading a story, builds our ability to find options in every situation. This makes humor an exercise that feels great!

What Makes You Laugh?

Think about times that you've really laughed—like maybe so hard you couldn't breathe or wiped a tear or had to call someone over to laugh with you. Circle the options below that most reliably make you laugh, give some examples, and add your own options at the end:

- Cartoons/Comics? Which ones? _____

- Stand-up Comedians? Who? _____

- YouTubers? _____

- Memes? Where do you find them? _____

- Movies? _____

- Humor Writing? _____
- Comedy Music? _____
- TV Shows? _____
- Great Storytellers? _____
- Websites? _____
- Puns? Knock-Knock Jokes? Anything with a lot of swear words? _____
- Watching people trip on stuff? _____
- What else? _____

Fantastic. I hope you had to go check some of those and you've been laughing while doing this important research.

Build Your Arsenal of Humor

What *else* might be hilarious? It's time to build your arsenal of activities, your journal of jokes, your handbasket of humor, your . . . OK, I'll stop. Think about the three people in your life who love to laugh the most. Call them right now and ask them where they get their laughs—what they watch, read, listen to—when they want to gut-laugh.

Person #1: _____

Where do they get their laughs?

_____

_____

Person #2: _____

Where do they get their laughs

_____

_____

Person #3: _____

Where do they get their laughs?

_____

_____

Now What?

Keep an eye out for the funny. Every time you laugh, you get more resilient in that moment.

Every time you find a new place to get some laughs, you build resilience skills for the future.

WOULD YOU LIKE FRIES WITH THAT?

PURPOSE: To stretch beyond our usual decisions.

Thirty-five thousand decisions. Most adults make about thirty-five **thousand** decisions every day. Does that sound tiring? No wonder we often repeat what we've done before (which is a decision, of course) rather than go through the decision process again. Habits develop because we make the same decision enough times that we allow ourselves to stop thinking about it.

Habits can be bad. Or good. That depends on whether the habit interferes with your being the kind of person you want to be. If it's your habit to start driving before putting on your seatbelt, that could interfere with being the alive kind of person you want to be. If it's your habit to go to bed without brushing, that could interfere with being the smiling kind of person you want to be. If it's your habit to stop at red lights, that can help you be the kind of person who doesn't go broke paying traffic violation tickets and higher insurance premiums.

Some habits aren't good or bad, just limiting.

What restaurants do you like? When you have the chance to eat out or grab takeout, what are your top restaurants?

1. _____

2. _____

3. _____

4. _____

What will you order there? Pick one of those restaurants, one where you usually get the same thing when you go there. Pretend I'm going to get you dinner. What's your order?

_____

_____

What else?

I text you. They're out of that! What else would you like? Go look at their menu online. Seriously, I'll wait. Go look at their menu and write down two other meals that you could get from there.

Option 1:

_____

_____

Option 2:

_____

_____

Might you enjoy it? How much do you normally enjoy your usual meal from this restaurant? (circle a number)

1 2 3 4 5 6 7 8 9 10

How much do you think you might enjoy one of your other options?

$$1 \quad 2 \quad 3 \quad 4 \quad 5 \quad 6 \quad 7 \quad 8 \quad 9 \quad 10$$

Good news! You don't have to order either of those meals. Just doing this exercise builds the skill of opening to change. Simply considering other possibilities—whether or not you actually try one—changes your perspective and gives you practice considering other outcomes.

Now What?

What other habits do you have that aren't harming you or helping you? Where else could you open to the possibility of a different outcome? Take the opportunity to develop this skill when you think of it, and try the next exercise to build this skill fast.

Look for options even when you don't think you need more.

Practice considering options will decrease your fear response to failure. The more choices you identify, the more resilient you will be in reaching your goals!

PICK A PICTURE

PURPOSE: To get more practice expanding joy in your life.

Finding possibilities is not useful only for problem-solving.

Imagine you're considering repainting the area in which you work. Whether you work in your living room or your cubicle or your garage, you might want a different color—or wallpaper (it might seem old-fashioned but some is pretty fun) or fabric wall hangings or laser lights. It's not a problem to be solved, but the more possibilities you find, the more likely you are to love the result.

Just like when we're struggling and can think of only one possible solution, we tend to limit ourselves in our pleasure as well. Taking the time to think of more ways to have fun, of ways to increase our joy, strengthens the skill of finding options.

Why Pictures?

I love to take pictures of flowers. The colors just lift my spirits, so I tend to take very close, saturated pictures. I take pictures of my kids because they *are* my oxytocin (that bonding chemical). My dog, the guy I love, my friends—I love to have pictures because I want to keep the feeling.

Looking at images changes our brain chemistry and strengthens our cognitive function. For example, looking at pictures of nature (as opposed to urban landscape) speeds recovery of the parasympathetic nervous system and lowers heart rate and blood pressure. All this calms the chemicals involved in fear and worry.

Remember those wall calendars with flowers or puppies that you might have seen behind a secretary's desk? Pleasing pictures of baby animals have been shown to improve our focus and attention and our ability to perform detail-oriented tasks for a period of time afterwards.

Pictures of people you love who love you back are almost as good for giving you that oxytocin rush (a chemical that makes you feel more connected and safe) as seeing the person in the flesh. This is so true that pictures of babies are used by lactation specialists to help moms produce breast milk when they're away from their baby.

Find a picture that pleases you. Which pictures make *you* feel good? Go right now and flip through your gallery for a picture that makes you smile or feel more relaxed. Describe the picture here:

_____

_____

_____

How often have you looked at this picture since you took it?

_____

How does it make you feel? Look at it again and name the feelings you get from it.

_____

_____

_____

Where could you put it?

We take lots of pictures that lift our hearts, and then we leave that feeling behind, or in our phone, and don't remember to feel the rush again by looking at it. Where could you put that picture you just described (or another one you love) so that you see it more often?

Circle the one(s) that sound best to you:

- Save it as the wallpaper on your phone.

- Print it and hang it on your bathroom mirror.

- Make it the lock screen on your phone.

- Ask your child to draw it, and stick it on the fridge.

- Make it your computer screensaver—or one of a bunch that rotate!

- Have it printed and framed and hang it in your office or your home.

- Print it out and stick it on the dashboard of your car.

- Recreate it in needlepoint or color by number or in an app.

- Have it printed on a mug or a keychain or a mousepad or . . .

Doing it makes a difference.

This exercise would be really easy to not quite finish. You picked the way you could see the photo more often, but will you actually follow through? As you'll see in the next section, taking action builds you up. So make a commitment to yourself and your happiness and check these off:

- Find a picture you'd really like to see more often.
- Decide how you're going to "post it" in your world.
- Do it right now or email the picture to yourself with your plan to make it happen.

You deserve this bit of joy!

Now What?

Seeing this picture each day will remind you to look for more ways to increase your joy. You'll look for more ways to boost your pleasure. Finding more options for happiness will build your resilience and make your life better each day!

YOU DID THAT!

HURRAH! You strengthened your resilience by finding options.

What are you planning on doing tonight? If something interferes, when is the next time you could do that thing?

_____

See how good you're getting at this?

Now for the Best Part

You've thought about a lot of things! Please follow this QR code by focusing your camera app on this code with your phone or tablet and clicking on the website that comes up.

Why would you do this?

Three reasons!

1. You may have thought of a creative option (or three) that no one else has, and others may have some great ideas for you.
2. Grab your badge!
3. **There's a gift** for you. We can't always afford to replace something when it's not serving us well, so grab these resources for making your car run better and longer, ten ways to get better cell phone reception, and more!

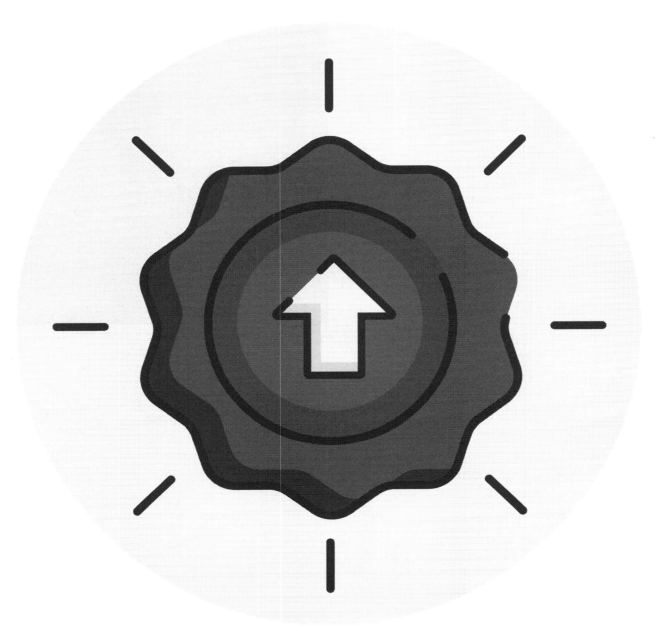

Take Action

TAKE ACTION

SOMETIMES OUR BRAINS SAY, "Taking action is more dangerous than staying where you are."

Very often, that's a lie.

When faced with a change, doing something—anything—different feels riskier than continuing on our current path.

Why does our brain do this? Well, it has to do with which part of our brain we're using.

The amygdala—a small but important section in the center of our head—is primarily tasked with processing emotions and memory. The amygdala is activated when we take action based on habit and is driven primarily by minimizing risk.

I asked patients with hypertension (fancy word for high blood pressure)—those who agreed to an intervention (taking medicine) and those who chose to take no action at all—if I could track their health and report back to them on hypertension-related health outcomes.

My group of patients mirrored what medical studies prove: taking a medicine to keep blood pressure in the normal range is much safer than making no change. It prevents the strokes and kidney disease, among other things, that my patients who didn't take a medicine experienced. My point was not to prove that though. My questions came after those health outcomes.

I asked the patients in the "nonaction" group what I could say, do, or show to a patient to help them take the action. I was told nearly the same thing by every person: "Remind them of other times that they've been hurt by *not* doing something."

The fear-based processing that comes so naturally causes people in the midst of change to freeze up. Your brain notices something is different, and you work to manage your discomfort, identify some options, and pick one to try . . . but your brain tells you it's a mistake. Don't do anything else that's new—you never know what could happen! So even though two people on the bus you're on are arguing and it's escalating, you don't get off the bus at the next stop because you're . . . stuck. It just feels safer to stay where you are, even if it isn't.

The ventromedial prefrontal cortex (I know, that's long and awkward; we abbreviate it vmPFC) is at the front of your brain, and it blocks some of that fear and helps us make decisions based on knowledge, data, and possibilities.

The vmPFC can look past your pounding heart, or the voice in your head saying, *"but that other thing could be dangerous too!"* and actually weigh your options, take in new information, and consider which risk is less likely to harm you.

Good news—you can control which one takes the upper hand in your decision-making!

The vmPFC is stimulated into action when you consider big ideas, like your own traits, preferences, abilities, and goals.

Thinking about the person you want to be is key to making thoughtful decisions that aren't solely based on habit or fear.

When you're in a difficult situation, or contemplating big change, it's much easier to stay stuck.

We need practice taking action. That way, even when we're uncomfortable and unsure, we have some muscle memory to help us engage our vmPFC.

That's why these exercises are crafted to help you consider your goals and then take some action in low-stakes situations.

YOU'RE AN ACTION HERO

PURPOSE: To utilize the skills you've already developed in taking action.

Trust Me

You take action all the time. Did you choose what time to wake up today and set an alarm? Did you pick out clothes and put them on? Did you eat something? Did you take your medicine or brush your teeth? You definitely opened this book and started reading! You've taken action already today.

Do You Suffer from Analysis Paralysis?

The answer is yes. Everyone does at times.

"Analysis paralysis" is the idea that a person gets so stuck in thinking about, feeling about, researching, or considering what to do that they avoid actually doing anything. Everyone postpones action at times. It's absolutely true that the skill of taking action is more of a struggle for some people than others, but the ability to take action (like resilience itself) isn't a character trait that just exists in some people and not in others. Everyone has actions that are easy to take and actions that make them pause.

I ask my patients to take action on a regular basis: start a new medicine, eat a different diet, exercise, wear a health monitor, get a vaccine, go for a test. Often the action I suggest gives my patient big hesitation. They'll agree but come back the next visit having not actually done the thing. They've thought, felt, researched, and considered but haven't yet acted.

Action means change, and all change is stressful.

Remember how our brains are skeptical of all change? Well, action (of any kind) guarantees change. So our brains resist, focusing on the potential loss, distrust, and discomfort of taking action, rather than the loss, distrust, or discomfort of doing nothing.

So the useful question isn't "Do you suffer from analysis paralysis?" The useful question is "What actions are a struggle for you and what helps you act anyway?" And to answer that question, we're going to jump in the Wayback Machine.

What Did You Do?

Think back over your life so far. You've taken some big actions.

What actions come to mind?

Think about different times or areas of your life. School, friendships, relationships, family, jobs, careers, travel, kids . . . name some actions you've taken:

_____   _____

_____   _____

_____   _____

_____   _____

(Fill the whole list—keep going; you've done a lot of stuff.)

Which actions stand out? When you look at that list, which three or four were the hardest for you to start?

_____   _____

_____   _____

How did you get going? What moved you to take action? Was it a deadline? Something you learned? A person who encouraged you? A reward that motivated you? Think about how you set yourself up to get started on something when it's a struggle. List strategies that have helped in the past:

_____   _____

_____   _____

_____   _____

Now What?

You are an action hero! You know a *lot* about how to motivate yourself toward action. Don't forget that you are already an expert in what doesn't and does work for you.

The next time you feel that stuck feeling or recognize that you're avoiding an action, follow these steps:

1. **Check your goal:** Does the action align with the kind of person you want to be? If not, your brain is right—don't take the action!
2. **Be kind to you:** Replace that negative self-talk ("why can't I just *do* this?") with empathy for your feelings and a little insight into your obstacle ("This *is* hard for me because _____.").
3. **Remind yourself what works for you:** You've overcome action-taking obstacles before. What do you know that might help?

In the following pages you'll do exercises that will give you more practice and strategies for the times when those three steps aren't enough.

VOTE

PURPOSE: To practice taking action, even when your ideal option isn't on the table.

What If You Were in Charge?

What if you could have a say in all the rules of society? What if your opinion were equal in value and impact to the opinions of all your neighbors for how your town should be run, what your high school uniforms should look like, and who the next leader of the free world should be? Oh right! It is!

As a matter of fact, your voice is more impactful than 60 percent of all the adults in the US in most of those decisions because only 40 percent of adults vote in most elections.

All of that is fascinating (to me) but a little off-topic for this book. Let's look at voting another way:

Voting Will Get You More Than Politics

What if you could do something several times a year that makes you more resilient? What if that thing were free? And organized by someone else? And took less than ten minutes? What if you could just show up and do the thing and BAM— you're stronger?

The Hidden Benefits to Casting Your Vote

When you vote, you take action. You may research, question, deliberate, or just shake your head beforehand, but you take a definitive action in that booth and it's excellent practice. You take that action with no guarantee of the outcome you want, without any assurance that the vote you cast—even if your candidate is successful—will bring about the results you wanted.

That's pretty much how all actions in life work, and it's the reason that many people get stuck.

We step up to take action and think:

"What if I lose something important through this action?"

"What if the person or initiative I vote for loses anyway?"

"What if the person or initiative wins but doesn't do/accomplish what I need?"

"What if they win and do the thing, but it ends up negatively affecting me and the people I care about?"

Sound familiar? That's loss, distrust, and discomfort coming back around in the Resilience Cycle. Action is hard because it causes change.

Taking action causes change. All change is stressful.

Remember resilience? The ability to navigate change and come through it with integrity and purpose. Often, action is required to do that. Like most skills, taking action gets easier with practice.

Look for VOs

VOs (Voting Opportunities) come up more often than you'd think. National elections occur every two years (yes, they do—midterms matter!), but local elections can be as often as twice a year. Don't feel ready for big-time political decisions yet? OK! Organizations run elections. Communities have votes. Your favorite brands run polls. Social media influencers ask for your vote daily!

Research three VOs coming up:

Get ready to Google.

When is the next national election? November _____, 20__
Are you registered? If not, register! https://www.usa.gov/register-to-vote

Who is running for something in your town and when? (Hint: search "your town" "elections" "20__")

Position: _____   Election date: _____

Position: _____   Election date: _____

Position: _____   Election date: _____

What groups do you belong to that vote for anything? Circle a few that you're a part of:

House of Worship   Kid's School   Apt Building/Condo/HOA

_____ Team   Book Club   Private Facebook Group

A Meetup   Service Org   Fantasy Sports Team

Any other group of adults I belong to!

Now find out something they're voting on, or put in some question to the group and ask for a vote.

Group: _____   Vote about: _____

Group: _____   Vote about: _____

Group: _____   Vote about: _____

What influencers or famous people do you admire? Name three who are active on your social media platform of choice:

_____   _____   _____

Follow them for a few days and wait for them to ask your opinion on something. Give it!

Now What?

Remember what we talked about in the introduction to this chapter? We discussed the push and pull of fear in our decision-making and how the trick to taking thoughtful action is to engage the vmPFC (ventromedial prefrontal cortex) by thinking. Voting, for most people, engages the vmPFC because we consider our goals before casting our vote.

Every single time you have a choice to make, you can practice this same skill by thinking "What do I want here?" before you vote—or take any action at all. In that way, every action you take can build your strength and get you closer to your goals!

DO ONE THING YOU DON'T WANT TO DO

PURPOSE: To feel the power and simplicity of action (after a bunch of planning).

Think about your work. Your paid work, your home work, your family work, or a volunteer project you run. There are the parts of it you love to do and the parts of it you avoid. There's something that has been on your mental (or written) to-do list for a while now that you just keep avoiding.

What is it that you have been meaning to do? Don't think too hard. Just write down the first thing you have been avoiding.

_____

What's terrible about it?
Seriously, if it were easy, fun, and fabulous, you'd have done it already. So what's the most uncomfortable part of it? Is it boring? Annoying? Painful? Does it involve talking to someone you don't like or doing something you hate doing? Be honest here—nobody is looking but you.

_____

_____

Do you need to do it?

One of the best things about being an adult is that you get to walk away from some tasks. Even when you're working for someone else, you can decide that something isn't necessary (sometimes). So think for a minute about this thing.

Does it need to be done? _____

Does it need to be done by you? _____

Do you have the information and resources you need to get started? _____

If you answered no to any of those, take the task off your list! You can delegate it, let the appropriate person know to reassign it, but it's not your action to take. Doesn't it feel good to get that off your list?

And if you answered no and took it off your list, go back to the first question, pick something else you've been avoiding, and go through this process again until you say yes to the questions above. Because now we're going to get it done!

How Do You Start?

There have been many books written about motivation and what it takes to be someone who gets stuff done. One theme that persists? Make it attainable and enjoyable.

Attainable

Making something attainable means turning the feeling of overwhelm and failure into something you know you *can* do. The best way to do that is to see the truth in that task you're avoiding.

The tasks we avoid are never just one task.

Monday To-Do List
1.   Check on timing Wednesday meeting
2.   Buy new printer cartridge
3.   Send proposal to XXY potential client (it was due last week!)

Can you feel the blood and sweat dripping off of #3? Are you positive that the first two things on that list will get done (as well as anything else I can think of to do) just to avoid even thinking about the third?

It's definitely the thing that needs to be done and done by me and that I *could* do that I have been meaning to do that I have not done and don't want to do!

What's so terrible about it? Well, I don't like writing that much and there are so many other things I need to do, and proposals take a while to write, but really the problem is . . . **they may say no.** That's *my* obstacle to sending proposals out the door—it's an invitation to rejection and that's terrible! Even while my entrepreneurial brain says, "If you never hear no you're not asking enough questions," I'm still no big fan of seeing potential partners walk away. It feels awful, and worse, it feels like my fault. I didn't know what to charge or how to clearly communicate the value of this work we could do together.

It's got to get done, and staring at it as one overwhelming task that invites failure is not helping. So my to-do list really looks like this:

Monday To-Do List
1.   Check on timing Wednesday meeting
2.   Buy new printer cartridge
3.   Send email to XXY to expect proposal in four days and gratitude for understanding
4.   Review notes from last call with XXY
5.   Get to next level on Clash of Clans
6.   Make list of XXY's three biggest needs
7.   Write one paragraph overview of proposed project with XXY
8.   Make Tuesday list of tasks for XXY proposal
9.   Send thank you to AAB from last week's event (remember the hula hoop!)

Baked into this list are three strategies I want you to notice:
1. None of these tasks takes longer than twenty minutes—attainable.
2. Each of these tasks are highly specific—attainable.
3. I end with something that I love to do and is entirely in my control—reward!

What is it that you have been meaning to do? What's the task that has you feeling overwhelmed, but it does have to get done, you do have to be the one to do it, and you have what you need to get started:

_____

When is it due?

_____

Is it already past due? If yes, send a short apology via text or email or phone call to the people most impacted (whether or not you explain is entirely up to you) and reset their expectation. Like this:

"Hi! This is _____. I wanted to let you know that I haven't forgotten about _____, and I apologize that it's not yet over to you. You can expect it _____."

Break it down. Way down.

When you look at that task, no matter how big or small, figure out the steps you need to get there. One way to do this is to imagine that your personal assistant (yeah, I don't have one either but _imagine_) is going to do each of these steps _for_ you while you lounge on a beanbag chair eating hot Cheetos. Write down each of the steps your PA would have to accomplish. Each step of data gathering, reaching out, writing, posting, ditch digging, whatever—be as specific as you can be. None of these tasks should take longer than twenty minutes. If they do, make them smaller.

1. _____

2. _____

3. _____

4. _____

5. _____

6. _____

7. _____

8. _____

9. _____

10. _____

11. _____

12. _____

(If you need more, add them!)

Now, what about the rewards?

Enjoyable

Our society has an underlying belief that work should be hard, that only children need fun to motivate them, and that enjoying your work means you are in some sense cheating. You're allowed to believe in your work and enjoy the idea of it, but if you're laughing and you're lighthearted and happy, you must not be at work.

Disagree!

You're a grownup—you get to decide when you get a gold star and the fun that goes with it. That's not lazy or silly. It's *effective*. Want to know why so many of us are drawn to distractions and procrastinations? Because that's how our brains get dopamine and oxytocin and all the chemicals that make us feel safe, satisfied, and sure of ourselves. Build *in* those moments and activities to your workday, and you can get all that neurochemical goodness **by accomplishing your work**. Drop the guilt!

Rewards

So, what things do you love to do? What makes you feel good? What would you look forward to? For practicality's sake, pick things that you can do from wherever you need to physically be to work on the task we were discussing above (the one you just broke into lots of little tasks) and pick things that don't need more than thirty minutes to enjoy.

1. _____

2. _____

3. _____

4. _____

5. _____

6. _____

Put the tasks and rewards together.

Go back to that twelve- (or two hundred-) step list and add in the rewards between certain tasks. You know your brain the best, so put them in where they'll do the most good and move you forward. Because, sadly, there is no personal assistant showing up to do all this for us.

Now What?

Do the first thing. Right now, before you turn the page. You've got this. Do it, and then scratch it out. Feel the feelings and have empathy for your own frustration or relief or boredom or fear. Manage your discomfort in one of the healthy ways you know, and...do it.

Did you do it? _____

How are you feeling? _____

JUST (YOU KNOW...) DO IT

PURPOSE: Practice taking action.

Schedule It

What appointment are you missing? There's an appointment you've been meaning to make. Circle the one(s) that come to mind or are overdue:

Annual Doctor's Visit	Dentist	Therapist
Physical Therapy	Teacher Conference	Haircut
Home Improvement	Car Inspection	Nutritionist
Vision Check	Create/Update Will or Life Insurance	

Something else _____

Who is it for?

Most adults are not only responsible for their own appointments. They help their kids, partner, parents, and others. So write down, next to the appointments you circled above, the names of the people you need to schedule the appointments for.

Who you gonna call?

Appointment You Need: Phone or Website: Next Time They're Open:

1. _____   _____   _____

     _____   _____   _____

2. _____   _____   _____

     _____   _____   _____

3. _____   _____   _____

     _____   _____   _____

Do it. Which one are you going to schedule right now?

_____

Great. Pick up the phone and call. If they're not open, pick up your phone or computer and schedule it online. If they don't do online scheduling, pick up your phone and put an alarm in for the next time they're open and you can call. When that alarm goes off, you can snooze it for five or ten minutes but don't turn it off until after you call and schedule the appointment.

Clean It Out

Somewhere in your home there is *that drawer*. It might be in your kitchen or the bathroom or your bedroom. It could be a whole closet or the top of your desk or counter. Somewhere there is a pile of stuff that you don't know what to do with exactly. You don't know that you need it, but you don't know that you don't need it either. So you've kept it, but you've also ignored it.

Where's your junk drawer?

_____

Whatcha gonna do about it?

It's time to clean it out.

Here's what you'll need:
- A trash bag
- A recycling bag
- A give-away box or bag
- A "keep" box

Follow these steps until the drawer is empty.

1. Take one thing out.
2. Decide if it's worth keeping (keep box) and where it should go in your home.
3. If it's not worth keeping, decide if someone else could use it (give-away box), if it can be recycled (recycling bag), or if it's garbage (trash bag).
4. Go back to step one.

Did you do it? _____ If you stopped in the middle, put an alarm in your calendar for when you're going to finish, and then come back to this page.

Now that you're done, do these four things:

1. Put the trash out.
2. Put the recycling out.
3. Put the giveaway in your car or by your door to get donated.
4. Walk around your house and distribute the things that you're keeping.

Reward yourself with something that feels great—you just took a _lot_ of actions!

Donate a Little Cash

What's a "little" cash to you? Is it one dollar? Five dollars? Twenty dollars? Twenty-five cents? Imagine walking down the street and realizing your wallet is open and your cash has fallen out. What amount wouldn't bother you that much? If you knew you only had $_____ in there, you'd just think "OK, bummer, but no big deal." (Fill in that blank with a real number.)

Great. I want you to donate that amount to an organization that you have never donated to before.

Pick a group.
What causes are important to you?

_____

_____

What organizations do you know of that serve those causes?

_____

_____

Which one would you like to give this little bit of money to?

_____

What's the website?

_____

Go do it!

What Was All This About?

Making appointments is a recurring task that often trips us up. It involves imagining our schedule ahead of time and committing to showing up. It often involves spending money and sometimes involves physical discomfort (or outright pain) or (even more intimidating) hearing bad news. So it's no surprise that making appointments is the number one task that people procrastinate. Doing it doesn't lessen our fear or discomfort around the task, but it does build the pathways for taking action.

Cleaning out a junk drawer is one task that requires you to take a hundred smaller actions. That is a way of doing some serious reps in the exercise of action taking!

Donating to an organization is another great way to practice taking an action. This action has small consequences for you but a ripple effect for the people served by that group and the people who give their time in its service. A new donor is valuable to them at any financial level because smart organizations leverage that growth to their other funders, using the number of donors (not only the total money) to prove their impact.

Now What?

Feel your feelings! You've taken a *lot* of actions in these activities, and you might be feeling a little sore after all that exercise. You have every right to feel however you're feeling. I hope you also feel proud.

The next time you have an action to take that is a struggle, remember that you do know how to do this!

YOU DID THAT!

GOOD FOR YOU! You strengthened your resilience by taking action.

Here's another idea for you about taking action. There are things we ought to do that never feel like they're necessary *right now*. There will be time for that later, we think. So—hard question—what is something that, if you were suddenly very sick, you'd wish you'd taken care of already?

Don't worry. There are resources below to help you do that thing you haven't done yet!

Now for the Best Part

You've worked on some tough concepts, and you deserve some kudos! Please follow this QR code by focusing your camera app on this code with your phone or tablet and clicking on the website that comes up.

Why would you do this?

Three reasons!

1. You can remind yourself of an action (or twelve) you took and see what others were inspired to do.
2. Grab your badge!
3. **There are gifts for you** to help you accomplish those "ought to do" tasks with a minimum of stress!

Persevere

PERSEVERE

PERSEVERE (PUR-SUH-VEER): to persist in any undertaking; to outlast obstacles while driving towards purpose, no matter the difficulty.

Sound Familiar?

Thomas Edison, Walt Disney, Richard Branson, Michael Jordan, Albert Einstein, George Steinbrenner, Steven Spielberg, Bill Gates (so. many. men.), Bethany Hamilton, Helen Keller, Oprah Winfrey. All mentioned over and over on "Inspiration" lists of people who persevered. We love to tell and hear stories of success after repeated failure because it *is* inspiring. These folks failed, often very publicly, and kept driving toward their purpose, with eventual success.

Have you noticed, though, that the answer to the question, "How can I keep going?" is often answered with inspiration rather than instructions? We experience failure, feel frustration or shame, and the only answer we can find is "Well, these folks did it. Be like them!"

This is inspiration. But *how* do we actually persevere?

A Personal Example

I've failed at lots of things, but the thing I've failed at the most often is fitness. In the course of my life, starting in my teens, I've tried dozens of times to get more fit, to build strength, endurance, tone, flexibility, and balance in my body. I doubt I'm alone in this, since three of the top ten New Year's resolutions every year have to do with striving for a healthier body.

I've failed at this slowly, and I've failed at it quickly. I've seen some change and success but felt a lot more apathy and disappointment. Unlike other things I've failed at and pretty happily given up on (writing poetry, rock-climbing, joining committees), though, I can't let myself off the hook here. I see too many folks every day who are suffering from pain, imbalance, and illness that fitness would prevent or postpone.

But man, trying *again* is hard!

The Answer Is (in Part) in the Definition

Some of the answer to "How can I keep going?" is in the definition of the word persevere. "To maintain **purpose** . . ." Reaching your purpose—whether it's a healthier body or landing a bigger client or improving a relationship—is the fuel that keeps us trying again. Reminding ourselves of the reasons we want what we said we want can get us to start again.

Check your purpose!

What if your purpose isn't on track? Trying again and again is a good idea *if your goal is still the right goal for you.* Persevering is crucial for resilience if it's helping you be the kind of person you want to be.

Imagine a college student who is doing well academically overall but has been struggling to pass Organic Chemistry. It's a required class in their science major, but they failed it sophomore year. They retook it junior year along with some humanities classes. They loved and excelled in Interpersonal Communications so much that they changed their major to Human Psychology. They're on track to graduate on time and well but so nervous and discouraged about taking Organic Chem *again!* We're all hoping that this student checks the graduation requirements, because Organic Chemistry likely isn't required for their new major, so perseverance in this way might not be useful—it might, in fact, be an emotional and financial drain for no reason at all.

The first step in using perseverance to be resilient is to make sure that your goal in a given circumstance is still aligned with your purpose.

Patience Isn't Enough

I always thought the reason I struggle with perseverance is because I'm so impatient. I want a solution *now*. I want it to work this time. I don't want to have to repeat something or do it over. A pattern feels like a rut to me by the third time I do it. I like doing new stuff, having new experiences—reviewing or editing or doing something over again doesn't feel as rewarding to me.

Some folks love repetition. They get a feeling of satisfaction from finding a routine that works for them and following it each day. Settling into a pattern in some areas frees them up for creativity or relaxation or challenges. And some folks feel that way about some routines and not others.

The reason for each of these varied reactions to repetition—and the key to controlling our ability to persevere when we want to—is the same neurochemical. Dopamine.

Here's the Science

Dopamine (a really tiny thing in the fluid in your brain) is a neurotransmitter. That's a molecule that passes messages between neurons (the communicators in your brain) to keep you alive and thriving.

Dopamine carries the messages to do all kinds of important functions.

We need dopamine for physical functions, including control of our heart rate, blood vessels, muscles, and kidneys. Dopamine plays an integral role in feeling and processing pain, and in our ability to sleep. Dopamine improves mood and attention, and it increases learning and motivation.

Why Is Dopamine the Thing?

Dopamine feels *great*. It's released when we eat a food we crave or when we have sexual pleasure. It's secreted when we get a compliment we value or feel a wanted, kind touch from someone we love. Dopamine is the brain's version of winning the lottery.

Some people get more dopamine from new experiences, and others get more dopamine from following a pattern they've followed before. Some brains—due to a multitude of factors—reward taking risk more highly, and other brains reward risk-avoidance.

Dopamine is the reward.

Using Dopamine for Good

Most often, the strategy of reward is offered only in the event of success. We define success as reaching our purpose or goal. Our brains know better though. Your brain gives you dopamine every time you do something it likes. It doesn't wait for the end of the day or the month or your life to say, "Good job!" We need rewards often to keep going.

Reward yourself for trying again!

Hopefully you're starting to recognize your own brain in this conversation. Wherever your brain is on the risk attraction-to-avoidance scale, you can still use this information to stick to a task or a goal.

My brain rewards me more when I try something new. So when I want to persevere toward a goal, I need to think about and focus on what's different this time. A new exercise, a different room in my house, a different time of day or music playlist or exercise partner or, or, or. If your brain rewards you more for consistency, focus on what's easily predictable or hasn't changed about your rededication to your goal.

You can use the good feelings you get from dopamine to motivate you to try again. When I find new music to listen to, that kicks my dopamine production higher even though I'm doing the *same* exercise routine.

> » A less risk-attracted person might reward their brain by going back to an exercise program they have done before and know well what to expect.
> » A less risk-avoidant person might reward their brain by finding a new place to run each day even though the run/walk pattern doesn't change much

Finally, the HOW: Patience + One New Thing = Perseverance

We've talked about how to turn up the dopamine to motivate ourselves. That increased motivation can serve to make us more patient. But patience alone isn't enough.

Perhaps you've heard this saying: "Insanity is doing the same thing over and over again expecting different results." If all we do is try the exact same thing over and over, we're unlikely to succeed, no matter how patient we are.

We have to change *something*. That's hard, because we all know how the brain feels about change. It's stressful! In order to have a chance at different results, though, we're going to have to look at:

- the purpose we're aiming toward,
- what we've tried before that hasn't worked, and
- what we know about ourselves and the situation . . .

. . . and find one thing to do differently.

For me, in my most recent attempt at fitness, I changed the expert I'm consulting. I found an affordable online trainer who is close to my age and incredibly encouraging (without being impressed by any of my excuses), and so far that one change is helping me stick to my goal. I'm a little stronger and a little more flexible, and my balance is improving. We'll see how it goes.

What are you failing at these days?

_____

_____

_____

Check your purpose. Is this still something you want to do? Does it align with the person you want to be?

- No? Let it go, Elsa. Let it go.
- Yes? Great. See below.

Be patient and find one new thing. Check something (or some things) below that you could change to improve your odds of success:

- Ask someone you haven't asked before for their support (build connections).
- Narrow your goal in some way (set boundaries).
- Try a solution you've rejected in the past (open to change).

- Find a thing you love to do that you can do while you work on this (manage discomfort).
- Reward yourself for smaller advances (set goals).
- Change the time or location or approach (find options).
- Do one thing toward this goal today (take action)!

See what I did there? All the skills you've been building throughout this book can help you persevere. And so can the activities in this section. Go get it!

WELL *THAT* DIDN'T WORK. OR DID IT?

PURPOSE: To identify perseverance opportunities and times to change your goal.

Failure Is Part of the Game

In American society we get a lot wrong, but one place where we truly excel is in seeing the value of failure. As a culture we agree that failure is necessary for success and that losing, falling down, and getting it wrong are all opportunities for learning.

What have you failed at?

Past or present, what did you try but not succeed at in your life? Think about after-school activities, sports, projects, goals. Did you start a band that got no gigs? Try a new job that didn't last long? Have an idea for an app that hasn't (yet) been developed? Fail to quit a bad habit or start a good one?

_____ _____

_____ _____

_____ _____

What did you learn? Now write down something you learned about each failure. What did you learn about yourself, your interests, your motivators?

_____   _____

_____   _____

_____   _____

_____   _____

If at First You Don't Succeed . . .

Not everything is worth doing. So the all-important first question in perseverance is: what is worth trying again and what isn't?

Zoom Out

Do you still see the value? When you look at that list of things you didn't finish, are any still appealing to you? Pick one or two past tasks or activities that you might want to attempt again.

_____   _____

Why do you still want that? What is the goal that you're trying to reach with that activity or task? What purpose does it serve in your life?

Task/Activity   Goal

_____   _____

Purpose:

Which of the above tasks or activities and the goal it's aiming for are aligned with the kind of person you want to be? Is it worth your time and effort?

_____

_____

_____

Now What?

Not every goal holds its value in your life. Some things we used to want or thought we should do fail to serve us. Trying again is not useful for its own sake.

Persevere only when it will strengthen you.

Before renewing your commitment to a goal, double check that your goal is still aligned with your purpose in life. Look to your failure for the lessons it holds and remember that you can learn something valuable whether you continue to pursue that goal or not.

DONE IS GOOD

PURPOSE: To test your purpose and to practice perseverance by completing an activity you stopped in the middle.

Quit versus Pause

In the last exercise we explored failure, how some offers lessons about how that goal isn't the right one any longer and how some offers lessons that can move us toward future success with that goal In other words, not every "quit" is a "fail."

What about the things we haven't decided to stop but we just haven't done recently? The things we haven't finished but we mean to get back to at some point? What can we learn from those, and how can they help us?

What have you paused? What have you started and not completed but you still might? Fill in some (or all) of these blanks:

Books: _____

Movie or TV Series: _____

TED Talk, Podcast, Article: _____

Online Course or Series: _____

A Class or Certification or Degree: _____

Promise to Someone: _____

A Craft: _____

Gift for Someone: _____

Photo Album/Baby Book/Memory Project: _____

A Home Improvement Project: _____

A New Initiative/Book to Write/Business to Start: _____

Language to Learn: _____

Now look back at that list and notice a few that catch your eye. Are there tasks or activities you really wish you had done? That still seem worthwhile to you? That bug you because they're left unfinished? Write those down here:

_____

_____

_____

Why do you still want that? What is the goal that you're trying to reach with that activity or task? What purpose does it serve in your life?

Task/Activity	Goal
_____	_____
_____	_____
_____	_____

Purpose:

Which of the above tasks or activities and the goal it's aiming for are aligned with the kind of person you want to be? Is it worth your time and effort?

Hit Play

Pick just one. You can come back for the others, but choose the one that's most aligned with your purpose and fits best with your current life, schedule, needs, and desires.

Which one will you try?

What do you remember about the last time you tried this? What time of day did you do it? How did you make time for it (or not)? Did you reward yourself? Did you enjoy it? Did you try to make it fun in any way? What was hard?

Patience + One New Thing = Perseverance

Patience is hard! Often we look back at an unfinished or abandoned goal and realize that we stopped because it felt like it was taking too long.

Why should you stick with this project this time? When you feel like dropping this project again (and you will), what do you want future you to remember? What will help you be more patient with it?

_____

_____

_____

What new thing will you add? What do you know now that you didn't know the last time you attempted this goal? Remember (or check out) the checklist at the end of the Perseverance introduction. What can you change in _how_ you attempt the goal this time to make your perseverance more successful?

_____

_____

_____

The Details

I have a friend who can't wink. He can blink, but his eyelids just don't work independently of one another. This issue comes up surprisingly often at parties. Upon hearing that he couldn't wink, people would _always_ do two things:

1. Wink themselves.
2. Say to him, "Try!"

As if "trying" hadn't occurred to him.

"Try" is not really a helpful strategy when someone hasn't succeeded in the past. We need specifics to accomplish something we haven't yet figured out.

What is the very first step toward this task you've chosen? Get specific with yourself. Look at the Set Goals section for help breaking this down into smaller tasks.

_____

_____

What do you need that you don't have for taking that step? How will you get it?

_____

_____

When (exactly) will you start?

_____

Did you put a reminder somewhere to do that?

How will you reward yourself for that step? Remember that rewards are your way of using your dopamine system for your own good.

_____

_____

How will you remember to go back to #1 and repeat this process?

_____

_____

For the Sake of Finishing

Will you finish this task this time? I don't know. But you can. If it stays aligned with your purpose and you keep advancing it, no matter how slowly, you can finish it.

Persevering builds confidence that we can keep going in any situation *we choose.*

Not every task is worth finishing. Practicing perseverance, though, builds our strength and resilience for the times we decide a goal is worth reaching.

Done is good, because it reminds us of our strength and our ability to persevere.

Now What?

Now you've reviewed the steps to take a task to completion. When you decide it's really what's right for you, you can. That doesn't mean you will—life may get in the way, or your goals may change. Resilience is navigating change and coming through it the kind of person you want to be. If you decide this goal is part of the person you want to be, remind yourself that it's in your power to make it happen.

A MATTER OF TASTE

PURPOSE: To practice perseverance in a low-stakes, high-frequency situation.

Perseverance Pain

If persevering were easy, we wouldn't be talking about it, right? So let's deal with the facts. It's often really uncomfortable—or downright painful—to try again. Repetition itself can be very uncomfortable.

Sciency Part

Growth often involves breaking down before we build up. To build muscle we must strain the muscle enough that individual fibers tear. When they grow back, they are stronger. The tearing hurts though. That soreness that you feel after strenuous exercise is a part of the growth process.

The physical pain of muscle growth is mirrored by the psychologic pain of neuron growth (learning), emotional growth, business growth, relationship growth, spiritual growth . . . most true personal and professional development is painful on some level.

There's a lot to help with this in Managing Discomfort, but there's also something new to learn.

Try Again Triggers

What makes you try again when you'd really rather not? We've talked a lot about purpose. Purpose is the fire inside that reminds us why our goal is worthwhile. It can be slippery to hold onto when we have ninety-eight push-ups to go and the first two were torture!

What makes you stop? What makes you give up trying again when something isn't easy? Consider a skill you tried to build that required repetition and think about what caused you to talk yourself out of continuing or to let yourself off the hook from persevering:

_____

_____

_____

What reminds you to try again? In addition to reminding yourself *why* you're doing this, what else do you use to trick yourself into going one more step? List as many strategies as you can think of. Page back through this section and the Managing Discomfort section for ideas.

_____

_____

_____

Perseverance to Change Your Mind

Everyone has foods they love and foods they don't.

What are some foods you've tried once or twice and didn't like?

_____

_____

_____

Picky Eaters Are BRAVE Eaters

As I mentioned in the Open to Change section, I'm not a brave eater. I've liked pretty much every food I've ever tasted. I don't have to be brave to try something new—I'll probably love it. Some people don't like most foods they try, so tasting something new requires serious courage. We call them picky but, if they eat anything at all, we should really call them courageous, don't you think? They've repeatedly tried foods, expecting to be totally disgusted, in order to find at least a few foods that are OK with them.

Even Taste Requires Repetition

According to the US Centers for Disease Control and Prevention, our tastebuds can require more than ten attempts to acquire a new taste. Did I mention that the brain distrusts change?

That offers us a great opportunity to try perseverance with a real chance of success.

What do you wish you liked that you don't? Is there a food that you don't like but is offered to you often? One that would make life easier if you genuinely enjoyed that taste? Something that you'd love to share with others but you haven't developed a liking for it? Look at your list above and choose one food you wished you did like:

_____

Ten Times in the Next Two Weeks

Seriously. Put this food on your shopping list! Look up a recipe or ask a friend who loves it to make it for you. Take as small a bite as you want, but come back here and record your reaction. See if you can get through all ten, even if you never develop a taste for the food. If you start to like it sooner, note when that happens..

Attempt #1: Date: _____ Reaction: _____

Attempt #2: Date: _____ Reaction: _____

Attempt #3: Date: _____ Reaction: _____

Attempt #4: Date: _____ Reaction: _____

Attempt #5: Date: _____ Reaction: _____

Attempt #6: Date: _____ Reaction: _____

Attempt #7: Date: _____ Reaction: _____

Attempt #8: Date: _____ Reaction: _____

Attempt #9: Date: _____ Reaction: _____

Attempt #10: Date: _____ Reaction: _____

Still don't like it? It's not for you! But also . . .

You can persevere despite some serious discomfort!

Now What?

What did you learn about you? Consider your obstacles to perseverance. Remind yourself of your "try again triggers" so that you know what to do when you do want to continue, but you're struggling.

FUN IS
THE WAY

PURPOSE: To strengthen our patience for the boring parts of perseverance.

How Do We Build the Patience Part?

We've been talking about how perseverance = patience + one new thing. And we've spent some time now figuring out what that one new thing is and how to keep trying new ways to get to our worthwhile goals. But what about that *patience*? For those of us who aren't inherently great at tolerating repetition (seriously impatient over here; how about you?), how are we supposed to find the patience that perseverance often requires?

Practice Practicing

A few years ago, I walked to an exam room for my appointment with a twelve-year-old boy who was there for a well child check. As I approached the door and raised my hand to knock, I could hear his voice raised inside. I dropped my hand and shamelessly eavesdropped.

"But *why* do I have to practice clarinet? I don't like it! You even said I can quit band after this year!"

And then I heard his father's—quieter, but definitely exasperated—voice respond, "You still have to practice! It's good for you. Don't think of it as practicing clarinet. Think of it as practicing . . . practicing!"

In that moment, this dad's brilliance struck me. Music, sports, math team, choir, or band—we rarely sign our kids *or ourselves* up for an activity because we think the next star is about to emerge. We do it for all the *other* skills that this one skill can teach. And one of those seriously important skills is practicing.

I took eight years of piano lessons, and today I don't own a piano. I do, however, know how to make myself sit down and do something for twenty or thirty minutes a day, even if I don't feel like it.

Practicing, even something we enjoy, is not always easy. We need practice at reminding ourselves why it's worth it, ignoring other things that need to or could get done, and finding the motivation and discipline to go back for another repetition.

Repetition increases our ability to persevere like running increases our exercise tolerance.

We have to find ways to practice practicing!

We're the Grown-ups Now

There are many advantages to being an adult. You *can* actually go to bed as late as you want. You can have dessert for dinner. And you can pick an activity to build your perseverance that is *actually fun for you!*

What would be fun for you? Consider a skill you want to build or an activity that you want to do better. First, pick several categories by underlining them here:

Sports	Musical Instrument	Language
Writing	Cooking/Baking	Visual Arts
Singing/Dancing	Body Strengthening/Fitness	Video Gaming
Cards/Board Games	Hiking/Climbing/Biking	Nature Watching
Gardening	Animal Training	Crafting

Something else you've thought of: _____

What's the goal? In this exercise, the purpose is to pick something you're not (yet) good at that you'd have to practice, something that you do not think you'd do well or get "right" in the first few tries. List your top four choices in no particular order:

_____   _____

_____   _____

What fits in your life?

Not all activities are created equally. Since you're choosing something that you don't yet know how to do well, you're going to need a guide of some kind: a book or an online class or a coach or a (kind, patient) friend to teach you. Think about the following (you'll actually answer these questions below):

- How will you learn it?
- How much time do you need each day/week for practice?
- Would you have to buy equipment?
- Do you need to create space to do this?
- When will you actually get started?
- **Will it be *fun* for you?**

Pick an activity that's a good fit for you right now, that's actually *fun* and that makes you more likely to get this practice in.

Choose your practice opportunity! Which one of the four activities that you were considering is the best fit for you right now?

_____

Congratulations! You've chosen a new hobby.

Now you're probably thinking, "Wait, what did I just agree to?"

What could you lose by doing this? Will you really do this? Is it really necessary? Do you *have* to do it? What won't you like about it?

Loss. Distrust. Discomfort.

I get it! Those are the brain's safety mechanisms, and choosing something new is a change.

You Have Choices

Just remembering that you have choices in this moment of change is a resilient act. So you've committed to yourself to try practicing, and you've picked a way to do it.

Is it still your goal to improve your perseverance? _____

If it isn't, then this isn't the activity for you. If it is, keep going.

Why do you want more perseverance?

_____

What is the value to *you* in practicing?

_____

_____

What do you need to start your new activity?

- How will you learn it?_____

- When in your day/week will you do it?_____

- What equipment do you need?_____

- Do you need to create a space for it?_____

- When will you start? _____

- How will you make it fun for yourself?_____

Put reminders in your calendar or on your to-do list to get everything lined up so you can get started.

Now What?

As you establish this new practice in your life, notice what's good about it and what's hard.

On the days you don't feel like getting to it but you do it anyway, learn what motivates you. How do you convince yourself to get started? What helps you keep going if it's uncomfortable or boring?

On the days you skip, ask yourself what obstacles occurred. What might you try the next time that obstacle comes up?

Remember that, whether you have found a lifelong hobby or just something to try this month, you are strengthening your perseverance!

YOU DID THAT!

LOOK AT YOU GO! You strengthened your resilience by persevering.

Are you staying on top of the whole reward idea? Do you reward your effort instead of just your accomplishments?

What's your favorite reward so far? _____

Now for the Best Part

You're crushing this process, and I want to celebrate that! Please follow this QR code by focusing your camera app on this code with your phone or tablet and clicking on the website that comes up.

Why would you do this?

Three reasons!

1. You can share a task you have let go of because it doesn't serve you and a goal you've found or rededicated yourself to reaching, and you can see what other people have learned about themselves.
2. Grab your badge!
3. **There's a gift** for you—a music playlist to keep you motivated when you want to persevere!

NOW WHAT?

With Integrity and Purpose

Over and over, throughout this book, I've reminded you:

Resilience is the ability to navigate change and come through it with integrity and purpose.

And yet, I waited until the end to explain that last bit. Why? Because those are yours.

Change comes at you from everywhere. Anyone can hand you a change. They dump a work assignment on you, run into your car, send you an unexpected bill, or tell you about a bad test result from a doctor's visit. They gift you a winning lottery ticket or send you an acceptance email for an amazing opportunity, invite you on vacation or throw you a surprise party. All that change—good and bad, expected or shocking—is stressful.

Integrity and purpose, on the other hand, are controlled by no one but you.

Integrity—wholeness, honesty to yourself, living true to your own values—the definition of all that and the execution of it are completely up to you. You get to decide what your own integrity looks like, and you get to change your mind when it's not working for you. Integrity is driven by your own beliefs and your own desire for authenticity.

Purpose is also entirely yours. You are the decision-maker in your life when the question is about your desires, your intentions, your goals. Other people will try to drive your purpose to align with theirs. You get to decide if their purpose is right for you. You decide the kind of person you want to be and what matters to you. In section 5 (Set Goals), the first exercise asks you to consider your priorities and offers strategies for matching those priorities—where you put your time and energy—to what you really want from life. We can't always control how our lives turn out, but we can completely control the purpose we drive toward and how we live as we try to get there.

You've learned that you can identify the truly unnecessary, unwanted stressors and walk away from them. You've discovered ways to identify both useful and unavoidable stress and use it to strengthen you. You've developed strategies for navigating the stressors you have to or want to face and be a little less winded by them.

You're more resilient and fit now than you were when you started this book.

You are ready to navigate each change and come through it with integrity and purpose.

How 'Bout Them Attributes?

Remember all that evaluating my team did to identify the building blocks of resilience? We found eight skills, and you and I have spent this whole book building those. We also found eight attributes:

1. Adaptability
2. Sense of humor
3. Self-efficacy
4. Empathy
5. Optimism
6. Confidence
7. Faith (in ideals)
8. Knowledge gained from past struggles and successes

Each of these is also an opportunity for growth and strengthening. As a matter of fact, you've likely grown and strengthened these attributes during each of the exercises you've accomplished in this book.

Think of it like the vitamins and minerals that are in the fruit you like to eat. The vitamins may not be why you eat the fruit, but they're a great benefit to doing something you wanted to do anyway.

Let's talk for a minute about each attribute, what it is, and how it strengthens your resilience.

Adaptability is the ability to adjust to different conditions or circumstances. The more adaptable you are, the less stressful you find a particular change.

Sense of humor is your ability to find something amusing in a situation. A plethora of research demonstrates the positive short- and long-term effects of using amusement and laughter to relieve stress and strengthen your body and mind in the face of change.

Self-efficacy is the belief that you can produce a desired effect. Knowing that you have control over some aspects of your life and that your own actions matter is crucial to recognizing the powerful role your own actions have on your life.

Empathy is the ability to identify and relate to the feelings, thoughts, or attitudes of someone else. Empathy aids tremendously our ability to create connections with others. Setting boundaries can be done without destroying relationships—and empathy makes that possible. Most of the resilience skills develop more smoothly when you have empathy for the impact of events on others.

Optimism is the tendency to focus more on the positive aspects of a situation than on the negative and to believe more strongly in the possibility of positive outcomes. Optimism is not necessary for resilience, but it aids strongly in opening to change, managing discomfort, setting goals that align with purpose, and persevering.

Confidence is belief in oneself, in one's powers and abilities. Confidence drives our willingness to set goals and pursue them by finding options. Confidence allows you to navigate change despite the obstacles and to know the value of your own integrity and purpose.

Faith is the belief in a set of ideas for which there is no concrete proof but much purpose. People who have loyalty to a concept have practice navigating change with a higher purpose in mind. Purpose does not come with guarantees or even guidelines, and faith of any kind strengthens a person's ability to persevere.

Learning from past struggles and mistakes is really the only sure way to find value in that pain and navigate future change more successfully.

Do You See Your Own Attributes?

As you read that list, did you find the attributes you've always had that aid you when you face change? Did you notice that you've grown some through these activities and experiences?

Here is a way to find out. Rate your own comfort with each from "That doesn't seem like me at all" to "Definitely me!" Put your first initial on the line wherever you fall for that trait at this point in your life.

Adaptability

(not like me at all)   (definitely me!)

Sense of Humor

(not like me at all)   (definitely me!)

Self-efficacy

(not like me at all)   (definitely me!)

Empathy

(not like me at all)   (definitely me!)

Optimism

(not like me at all)   (definitely me!)

Confidence

(not like me at all)   (definitely me!)

Faith (in ideals)

(not like me at all)   (definitely me!)

Knowledge Gained from Past Struggles and Successes

(not like me at all)   (definitely me!)

If you're curious, go back to Chapter 6 of the Introduction—Learn Resilience on Purpose—and see how your answers compare!

Seriously, Congratulations

Congratulations is a word that merges the concepts of giving thanks and wishing joy.

We've spent a bit of time together. You've done a lot of work. You've learned about your brain, about yourself, and about what you want and how to get it. Whether this book was full of new ideas or mostly reinforced what you'd already noticed about yourself and the world, you deserve genuine congratulations.

You've been through a bunch of stressors since you first opened this book. You stopped and started it at least a few times while you navigated the other demands on your time. You navigated a lot of change and yet . . . you kept this purpose—moving yourself from stressed to resilient—as a part of your focus in order to strengthen yourself.

Together, we've created an algorithm—a set of steps for solving a problem—for... everything: every challenge you face, every opportunity you discover, every change that comes.

1. **Notice your safety reflexes.** Don't be offended or frustrated—your brain is just trying to keep you alive. So acknowledge the potential loss, the distrust, and the discomfort. Have empathy for yourself!

2. **Are you in danger or just uncomfortable?**
   a. If you're in danger, focus on *that* and fix what you have to fix to be safe.
   b. If you're uncomfortable, manage your discomfort in neutral or positive ways.

3. **Is this change necessary and/or useful?**
   a. If neither—walk away.
   b. If either . . .

4. **Remember that you have choices.** You always have choices for where you put your actions and your focus.

5. **Consider your integrity and your purpose.** What kind of person do you want to be in this situation? What are you driving toward. Set your goal.

6. **Find options and try some until you reach your goal.** All this action is change, and change is hard. When it feels too hard, go back to number one and start again.

I'm thankful that there are people in the world willing to work toward strength in between all the tensions in their lives. I'm thankful for you. And I'm wishing you joy in a more resilient experience of life.

Congratulations!

I'LL MISS YOU! UNLESS...

WE'VE BEEN THROUGH A LOT TOGETHER. You've trusted me with some of the hardest and proudest moments of your life and been really honest in these pages.

I'd like to stay connected. Would you?

Please follow this QR code by focusing your camera app on this code with your phone or tablet and clicking on the website that comes up.

If you've created your avatar, come mark yourself complete and check in with others who've finished the book. If you haven't been online yet, I hope you'll say hi and grab the badges you've earned by doing this work—as well as all the **free gifts** that are waiting for you.

You can contact me there also and stay connected for future conversations or questions. I'd love to be one of the connections that strengthens your resilience in the months and years to come. Thank you for trusting me with your stress.

ACKNOWLEDGMENTS

Jess Ponce, manager and brilliant mind, true friend and truth-teller. Without him, I would definitely never have sat down to write this book. He definitely made me do it. Thank you, Jess, for your tireless work and excellent counsel. It's written, and you were probably right.

My sincere thanks to Julie Haase and Emily Hitchcock and their teams at The Writer's Ally and Storehouse Media Group. I had words. Thank you for making them into an actual book.

Dave Shrein and co. at The Blocks Agency, thank you for seeing all the ways this book could be an experience and for helping me to create the images to make it real, and the gathering place for this amazing community.

To Lisa Bloom, Danny Iny, Bhoomi Pathak, and the Mirasee world that you guide so skillfully, my thanks for your curiosity, your support, and your clarity.

To Patty Block, Michael Roderick, and Jason Van Orden—you three are, separately and uniquely, wonderful mentors who have helped me see the multitude of ways I can do the work that has chosen me.

Matt Diabes and Benny Cooper, Laurie Weingart and the whole team at Tepper, I thank you for devoting yourselves to the larger questions of work and finding the answers that allow us all to do what we do while being who we want to be.

Jen Carl and Carlota Madriz Lanao, I appreciate each of you and the tremendous amount of patience and skill it takes to keep me running on time and in the correct directions.

Raven Disalvo-Hess, you were the first person to read the book beginning to end—and it's stronger for your perspective and suggestions. Thank you for your candor and your compliments.

To Ari, Nadav, Oren, and Gavri, who encouraged me to keep writing, never once expressing skepticism about this book that seemed to be taking forever. For all the times you found me at the coffee shop instead of home, got your own meals (and cooked for each other) while I worked on it, and helped out with extra chores so I could get back to it. I promise to support your dreams as truly as you've supported mine, always.

To Jesse, thank you. For all of it, but especially for knowing I can when I'm not so sure and for being proud but not too impressed. You make all the difference.

Dad, thank you for always being a bit surprised by what I'm doing and also completely positive there's nothing I can't do. I love you.

To my people. You make our houses into home for me and my boys and make our neighborhood into community. Renee, Jonathan and Vita, Eitan, Akiva and Adi, Jaci and Daphne, Keren and Jeremy, Marisa and David and Leo and Ruthie, Phyllis and Joe, we couldn't end each week without you.

Beyond all these incredible folks, there are some women who are there whenever I ask and very often even when I don't.

Rachele, if I've got this, it's due to you.

Sharon, you never run out of room in your heart or time in your day when it counts.

Ilana, thank you for asking, always, and caring about the answers.

Liz, I simply couldn't do all this without you.

And now, the thank you I have thought about every page of this book: you. Thank you to each of you for engaging in this work, for reading and questioning and working towards the version of yourself you most want to be. I'm lucky and grateful for all the people I've met who've shared struggles and stories and challenges as yet untackled. Thank you for your purpose, your patience, and your trust. I hope to hear from you as you navigate whatever changes come next!

NOTES

CHAPTER 4

1 "The World's Broken Workplace," News, Gallup, accessed Dec. 2, 2021, https://news.gallup.com/opinion/chairman/212045/world-broken-workplace.aspx.

CHAPTER 5

1 "Resilience" Oxford English Dictionary, ed 12.4.191.https://www.oxfordlearnersdictionaries.com/us/definition/english/resilience.

CHAPTER 6

1 "Our Services," News, Stanford University, accessed December 2, 2021, https://news.stanford.edu/news/2007/february7/dweck-020707.html

EXERCISE 7

1 "How to Be Happier at Work—3 Tips," Top Stories, Inc., accessed December 2, 2021, https://www.inc.com/minda-zetlin/how-to-be-happier-more-calm-googles-happiness-guru.html.

ABOUT THE AUTHOR

WE HAVE BEEN TOLD to "avoid stress" so much that experiencing stress feels like its own failure. Resilience expert Deborah Gilboa, MD, aka "Dr. G," works with families, organizations, and businesses to identify the mindset and strategies to turn stress to an advantage.

Renowned for her contagious humor, Dr. G inspires audiences with her illuminating stories and provides no-nonsense prescriptions for character development. She works with groups across multiple generations to rewire their attitudes and beliefs toward a common objective and create resilience through personal accountability and a completely different approach to stress.

Dr. G is a leading media personality seen regularly on Rachael Ray, TODAY, and Good Morning America and is the Resilience Expert and a guest co-host for *The Doctors*. She is also featured frequently in the *Washington Post*, the *New York Times*, *Forbes*, and countless other digital and print outlets.

Dr. G is a board-certified attending family physician in practice at the Squirrel Hill Health Center since its founding in 2006 and is fluent in American Sign Language. In addition to being a graduate of the University of Pittsburgh School of Medicine (where she is also a clinical associate professor) and Carnegie Mellon University, she is an alumna of Chicago's Second City Improv Theater.

Discover why Dr. G consistently receives "Top Rated Speaker" at conferences and business events around the world at askdoctorg.com/speaking.

If you'd like more support along with free resources, click any of the QR codes in this book or visit askdoctorg.com.

Dr. G lives in Pittsburgh with her four sons (when the oldest are home) and Yofi the wonder dog.

If you'd like to contact Dr. G, don't hesitate. You can reach her at info@askdoctorg.com.

Made in the USA
Middletown, DE
18 August 2022

71674876R00135